Winter Jasmin

Poems of Life
Conflict, Nature, Love,
and Faith

S.K. Haddad

Clink
Street

London | New York

Published by Clink Street Publishing 2017

Copyright © 2017

First edition.

ISBN: 978-1-910782-16-3
E-Book: 978-1-910782-17-0

To my dear friend Sandra

Table of Contents

Life and Death

When Time Trampled on her Head

Beyond the city alleys,
Where golden food crops grow;
Within the glens and valleys
Where waters edge and flow,
She picked the blood red poppies,
The slender drops of snow.

I answer if you ask me:
"Has beauty's crown been won?"
'Look not to the apple tree
Which blossoms in the sun:
Beauty, dressed in flesh, could see,
Could talk and leap and run.'

Like jasmine of the orient
She filled the soul with glee:
Nimble, youthful and salient,
Bright, vivacious and free,
Her face was far more radiant
Than sun beams on the sea.

When time trampled on her head,
It plucked its hair quite thin;
Eyes turned dim and ears like lead
With bristles on her chin;
Her face, like a ruffled bed,
Showed sunspots on the skin.

Age worked hard its cold steel mill
And crumpled her pure brow;
With its creeping perfect skill
It caused her back to bow;
In her features one sees still
Signs of past beauty now.

She waits for death to vanquish
Her body in its hold;
Her legs, once pretty, languish
Beneath her weight and fold;
Heaven will have no anguish
But streets of light and gold.

You Slipped Away

You slipped away
Out of your warm glittering light,
You slipped away
Into your cold and moonless night;
You left without saying goodbye,
You did not smile, you did not cry:
You simply walked out, slipped away.

You left us and you felt no pain,
Nor will you come to us again.
Where is your earnest tight embrace?
The knowing look, the tender face?
The mundane plans and the surprise?
The loving twinkle in your eyes?
All was lost: you slipped away.

You pay no heed to call or sound
Nor to appeals from all around;
You left us while you stayed at home,
You walk from room to room and roam,
You do not seem to care at all
Whether we die or rise or fall:
You slipped away in your mind.

You shuffle as your lose your way
In your own home by night and day,
Then stumbling fall and cannot rise:
The spider crawls, the hornet flies,
But you remain upon the ground
Not crying or making a sound
You slipped away in your mind.

I slipped away
Out of your memory and care;
I slipped away
You know not when, you known not where:
As if I am no longer there;
You look at me, but do not see
How you prided yourself in me:
I slipped away from your mind.

You are not bothered if I creep
Or crash a glass jug as you sleep;
Although I see you, thin and frail,
My love for you will never fail.
The time will come when we will meet
Renewed before our Saviour's feet
When this sad world slips away.

The Obese

He steadily increased in weight,
It was his nature to be great:
But can his big heart tolerate?
Will not his belly ulcerate?

His friends pretended to be wise:
Each one was eager to advise;
His figure could bear no disguise
Nor he the portents of demise.

"Check your cholesterol level,
Fats and uric acid gravel,
Thin your blood sugar with a shovel,
Must death join you on your travel?

"Attend a slimming club and train:
We bet you will be thin again,
Begin to lose a stone or twain:
Your fat will slither down the drain."

Was that all their conversation
Just to increase his frustration?
Bigger men are in the nation
Who feel greater consternation.

His friends all died in turn, each one,
But he outlived their jokes and fun
And when his life on earth was done,
He said his farewell to the sun.

It was when he, an old man died,
One digger to another cried:
Make sure the gave is deep and wide,
This man is big from side to side.

The Cattle Market

Some people in the West and East
Count a woman a market beast,
Or a Jersey cow at least,
With flesh to yield a wholesome feast.

She is too plump to be a bride:
Her skin is best suited for hide!
They look upon her and deride,
Judging her figure short and wide.

Fine features, but her nose is big,
Her hair looks like a painted wig!
What stocky legs, rump of a pig!
What voice! just like a breaking twig.

How lovely is her smiling face,
A spring of happiness and grace,
But that dark mole is out of place
Like a foul spot upon white lace.

With his brain, as sharp as a knife,
He seeks for one to share his life;

He can face men in peace and strife
When he proudly shows off his wife.

I have known people in my time
Who sought a young wife in their prime,
Counting themselves truly sublime.
Choosing between the quince and lime.

Beauty is skin deep, it is said,
Time creeps upon its neck and head:
Some folk will wake one day in bed
To find their gold a mass of lead.

True beauty lives within the soul:
Heart to heart will forever call,
It breaks down fences, strong or tall
To be in love the all in all.

Look on the heart, not on the crust,
The charm of person, not the bust
On things that will endure you lust
When all else crumbles into dust.

The Desert

Stretching out beyond man's eye
As if to eternity,
Yet of this world much a part
In danger, serenity.
Of the landscapes of the earth
Is a special entity:
Mother of energy, might,
Bed of death and enmity,
Queller of man, unconquered,
Proving his mortality,
Yet he finds rest for his soul
Within your tranquility.

Your dunes, as gentle ripples
Of the deep waves of the sea,
Unfixed and ever changing,
Beckoning, calling for me,
Yet at times blown and blasted
Into heaven to be free,
Like a sea storm on your face
Where death and fury agree;
Life becomes gravely threatened,

Man trembles and bends the knee
As he cries for God's mercy
That danger may pass and flee.

I love you, not for the oil
Buried deeply in your land,
Nor that stars in the dark night
With luculent brilliance stand,
But that my father did earn
A living from your harsh hand,
Not seeking riches, but life,
Meek was his honest demand
Until his life was ended,
Until he, at God's command
Slept in earthen grave beneath
Your fervid and sun-baked sand.

One day I took my mother
To visit him where he lay,
She stood alone, bewildered,
Not knowing what words to say;
Lonely and broken by time
Where silence vanquished the day.
Her lips quivered tenderly,
She appeared intent to pray.
The grave stone had subsided
Beneath the weight of decay;
I wondered when the desert sand
Will erase its marks away.

Desert Death

He lost his way and could not find it back;
The wind erased the marks of his one track:
His car ran aground in the sandy dunes
While he listened to jolly radio tunes;
No man passed, no buzzard or curlew
But snakes and flies and deadly scorpions knew:
His bones were picked as if polished by hand
As he decomposed in the heated sand.
Great was his courage, short his earthly run:
His mother lost a noble elder son.

The Dingle

I walked through a valley dingle
Where trees embraced above my head
Forming a lacework that mingled
With piercing spotlights widely spread;
I strode on the path I singled,
Upon branches and twigs long dead.

In the solitude of silence
I pondered on nature's design,
Felt the rustling leaves and presence
Of the oak tree and wayside pine
Where the shrubs entwined in semblance
Of hands begging the light to shine.

I soon had reason to regret
The use of nature as a pan
As I saw a reeled out cassette,
Newspaper, glass, an empty can,
A disembowelled radio set,
Plastic and the refuse of man.

Uncle Evan

Oh, take me to the graveyard,
Let me see the stone
Where he laid his weary head,
Where he sleeps alone.
He walked up ahead of me
On that solemn hill,
Then stood against the grave,
Motionless and still;
No words were said between us,
Each reviewed the past,
But I knew that tenderness
And grief held him fast.

We stood there remembering
One who grows not old.
It was before the Winter,
But the wind was cold;
No tears escaped from our eyes:
They were trapped inside;
Not so with the cloud that passed
By the Welsh hillside:
It wept hard upon the grave

And upon our head,
Spoke the language of the heart,
Said what should be said.

His chest narrowed upon him
Exhausting his breath,
Till at fifty seven years
Relief came in death.
His dear father, my uncle,
Inhaled the coal dust
Until his lungs were shattered,
As if lined with rust.
What could one say on that hill
In the south of Wales?
Is there need? The Autumn wind
Comes each year and wails.

Mrs. Hughes

In the small town of Tregaron,
Between valley and meadow,
Bryntirion sheltered the aged
Whose life was a bare shadow.
One lady there was ninety four,
A widow of long standing,
Wizened and thin, wrinkled and old,
Failing in understanding.
Her memory of the present
Lasted for a brief moment,
But childhood days returned afresh,
Were happy, free of torment.
Most friends had died, those who remained
She could barely remember,
As if the calendar of her days
Had marked early December.
Not knowing how to gather words,
She muddled and threw them out;
Despite the lostness of her thoughts
Her features were stern throughout;
She said: "Now only John and I

Are left to live together",
Her John had slept for many years
Beneath the soil and heather.

The Village Church

Kneel my soul, before the service starts:
There is time to remember
The common fire in our souls and hearts
That left a single ember.

One large family in bygone days,
We went to church together
And raised our voices in hymns of praise
In fair and stormy weather.

Our parents joined the singing aloud:
Though small, we tried to follow,
Were told that we should never be proud
Nor should our hearts be hollow.

As children we rushed to Sunday School
To hear of Jesus the Lord;
We learnt of the wise man and the fool,
Had no reason to be bored.

My father called us daily to pray
While falling upon our knees,

But Sunday was a most holy day
As the bell rang through the trees.

Lonely church, wounded by time, it stands
Amidst elm trees and oak
Which scattered sunlight that fell in bands
On Revered Morgan's cloak.

Its metallic spire with sabre point
Reached upwards toward the sky
To lift our eyes to Heaven and point
To our blessed home on high.

O quiet Graveyard with grey on green,
How sadly I often stood
Where primroses, daffodils were seen,
The cuckoo chimed in the wood.

When small, I wondered how bodies slept
In the restful arms of death,
Their spirits gone to God to be kept,
Transported by their last breath.

Within the church my sister married
The man she loved so well
And in the grave we came and buried
Her frame which in childbirth fell.

Her wedding bells, which shattered the air,
Then rang their mournful slow knell;
How I miss you my sister, most fair,
Much more than verses can tell.

My elder brother ventured to make
A living in the city,
But he did not utterly forsake
The home of love and pity

Where compassion manifestly showed
In fire, teapot and kettle,
Where God's love made our home its abode
In grounds with sheep and cattle.

Dare I remember them and not weep
For parents sisters, brother?
For my small sister in death's long sleep
Who fell amidst the heather?

Their bodies are here, their souls are found
Resting in our Defender;
I love that parcel of sacred ground,
My bed when I surrender.

The Reaper

Pass O Reaper, pass me by,
See, I am no longer fresh,
Fat and flabby is my flesh,
Hard my hearing, dim my eye,
Pass O Reaper, pass me by.

I shall pass, but will return
When your flabby flesh will rot
Like a rump broiled in the pot,
Better if your dust will turn
Into ashes when you burn.

Sharpen blade when you come back,
Let the cut be swift and clean,
Be the craftsman when you glean;
I do not think that you lack
Practice when you strike and hack.

Give me sleep, let me not see
Your sharpened steel gleaming bright
As it cuts me from the light;
Take my body, set me free
While true life beckons to me.

Autumn in New Jersey

I spent the evening in the porch
Upon a swinging chair
While the soft breeze caressed my face
And told me it was there
To cool and comfort my sad brow
And circulate the air
As maple trees, painted with blood,
Waved with a fiery flare.

The carefree birds on bough and branch
Shared tunes with some unseen
While in the porches pumpkins stood
Ready for Halloween;
Motorcyclists rode up the street
Each proud of his machine:
A thumping Harley-Davidson
Spotlessly polished, clean

Nature's autumn, autumn of life,
Marches to signalize
That winter's night will surely come

To bring tears to our eyes;
The breeze, the sigh, the breath of life,
Fluent without surmise,
All said, my mother's star will set
Before the next sunrise.

The Funeral Director

It is quite strange how men presume to live
For endless years when none can truly give
That certainty that his days will be long,
That death has ceased from subduing the strong.

There lived a man in a modest Welsh town,
An undertaker of some great renown;
Men came to him to have their dead interred
In graves, or be cremated if preferred.

I went to ask how he ordered his trade
In case the time came when I needed aid;
He showed me schedules of varying price,
Suggested I book while the cost was nice.

He then bragged of how many men he placed
Within the ground, whom death pursued and chased,
Famous people, well honoured in the land
Who passed through his parlour under his hand.

"I buried this one and I buried that,
Buried all kinds, the lean and the fat,

Provided a service, sombre and clean,
Partnered my father when I was nineteen."

He mentioned by name a knight of the queen
Whom he buried when death ruptured his spleen,
"His brother remains, you can guess,"he said,
"Who will bury him when he drops down dead".

I was amazed how he dared to presume
That he will last before meeting his doom
When he was in his seventy ninth year
Standing at death's door, living in its sphere.

Mrs. Jones

She lived alone in a house of stone,
My neighbour for countless years,
Widow forlorn, no one to own
Yet sheltered away her tears.
The day was hot and I did not
Consider lighting my fire,
But I did spot her chimney pot
With smoke rising up higher.
I rang her bell, my pulse did swell,
I worried she caught a chill,
But I could tell that all was well:
She seemed too bright to be ill.
She looked and turned, the coal fire burned
The hearth was covered with dust,
The hot air churned, Summer returned
To discomfit the robust.
I asked her why the flame was high
On a day, warm as could be;
She was not shy of her reply:
"It is company for me".

The Kid

My dear mother sang a story,
Full of pain and grief and woe,
Of a lady, poor and hoary,
With a tune that I still know.

Let my chant incite a notion
With its sad and mournful key
Of my feeling and emotion
When my mother sang to me.

This stout lady, old and lonely,
Kept a kid, a little goat,
Not for meat, but friendship only,
Never thought to hurt its throat.

She lived by a rugged hillside
With the kid to share her life,
Kept its manger by her bedside,
Never showed it a bare knife.

It was gentle, fairly coated,
With a greyish tint throughout;

She was loving and devoted,
A good woman, without doubt.

But the kid one early morning
Sought for pastures far from home,
Heedless of her constant warning
Not to wander, not to roam.

Then the wolf descended quickly
With ferocious speed and skill
And it slew it, rather quickly,
Such the nature of the kill.

She awoke to gather firewood,
Missed the kid and called its name,
Searched the wilderness and far wood
Till she hobbled, sore and lame.

Then she saw disordered fresh bones
Mixed with clot and skin and hair
Scattered amidst dusty rough stones,
Hooves and horns, she found a pair.

She lamented with a harsh cry
And her eyes began to smart:
Woe to me, oh, woe, I must die,
Wolves have devoured my heart.

The Dancer

It was late, we sat alone, my hands in a clasp,
His elbows on the table, a glass in his grasp;
I tried to know him better as he drank and smoked,
As he conversed most wisely, though he
coughed and choked.
I lived far away from home having left when young,
But when I paid a visit, boasted with my tongue,
Trying to impress him with proud notions I had,
But he was to make me feel like a shameless cad.

The television glared, we viewed from time to time
Though a distant town clock chanted the midnight chime.
An image filled the screen, began to sing and dance;
I said with derision and with a haughty stance;
"Look father, a clumsy lump, listen how she sings,
A woman without grace, a plump bird without wings".
His words were a reproach which I cannot outlive:
"She waves like a banner because she wants to live".

Folly

How does new life shoot from the dust
Where dead bones lie with wood and rust
Nauseating stench beneath the crust?
There time abandoned hope and trust,
Dead is desire, as honour lust,
Weak men, untrue and others just
Decomposing most hideously?

The tiny seed will grow to make
A large tree when its shell will break,
Cleaving the earth when Spring does wake.
It forms the wood for bed and stake,
The handle of the pick and rake,
For fire to burn and sparks to flake:
The soil becomes these wondrously.

From seed, too small for eyes to see,
Comes a child from the inner sea,
Crying for breath on mother's knee;
More helpless than the calf is he,
Yet stronger than the ox will be,

Is part of nature, part of me
And part of mankind truthfully.

Watch how the grain of Summer's wheat
Will turn to bread sold on the street;
Likewise the babe must grow and eat:
Milk turns to skin and bones and meat,
To growing brains and growing feet
And is transformed to life and heat,
To flesh and blood most readily.

Thus, from elements, mean and weak
A man is formed to cry and speak
With tongue fierce as an eagle's beak.
Riches are his to search and seek;
He stands upon his ego's peak,
Defies the proud, abhors the meek,
Despises all men haughtily.

Where creatures of the soil are found,
His body shall be boxed or bound
And left six feet within the ground,
Silent and still without a sound,
Rotting beneath a raised up mound,
The graves are full, the dead abound:
They had to go unwillingly.

And does not Folly utter lies
That when death comes to close men's eyes,
Each one, like meaner creatures dies
Without punishment, without prize?
Its children think that they are wise:
The fool looks for shadows and sighs
When none shall live eternally?

Men scoff at God with their replies,
Yet they shall find to their surprise
That they, like all the dead shall rise
To stand before the One all wise
And answer for their guilt and lies.
Lord, must one hear their wildest cries
When they perish eternally?

Pride

Clay upon hardened clay has walked,
He opened wide his mouth and talked,
A stench escaped from a jar uncorked.

He talked as if he would not die,
His tongue defied the earth and sky,
But his clay within the clay shall lie.

All life is mine, he proudly said,
The living now as were the dead,
Yet he cannot sow hair on his head.

He did not earn his looks or mind:
Gifts come from God for He is kind
And showers His blessings on mankind.

Self-esteem blinds his mind and will,
Each day he grows haughtier still,
But a virus can seize him and kill.

His vain body may dance and sway,
A clot of blood his heart may slay
For worms to consume him in the clay.

As a lion outside the den,
He lives his three score years and ten,
Like beasts shall perish, not knowing when.

He forgets God and does not think
That in death's lap his life small sink
Until the grave vomits out his stink.

Many a beauty once had been
That wizened when death's face was seen,
Eyes closed in darkness that once were keen.

Riches halt not the stride of time,
He shall lie in the clay and lime
Without a penny, without a dime.

O lump of clay, arrogant, loud,
Before your birth time kept your shroud,
The wriggling worms shall feed on the proud.

When I was Young

I did not fear the flying bomb,
The wailing sky, the burning store,
Nor death that walked along the road,
Came through the roof, entered the door
And left us dying on the floor:
Such was the nature of our life
Throughout the dark years of the war
When I was young.

I did my part for my great home:
It was my love, I fought and tried
To help the fallen by the way,
The little ones who gasped and died
And mothers who shed tears and cried.
I went about with upright back:
I did not fear the raging tide,
When I was young.

When illness left my body torn,
I had a will to battle through,
When hardship overwhelmed my life
And hunger pierced my belly too,

I did not learn to wail and rue,
But kept my head raised to the sky:
Courage, my twin, beside me grew
When I was young.

I bravely sailed upon the waves
And climbed the mountains dressed with snow;
Camped in the woodland at nightfall
And heard the wind's loud sirens blow,
I watched the river swiftly flow,
Rode on its back with my small boat;
Was proud of cuts my flesh did show
When I was young.

Now I fear the bustling high street,
I dread to buy a loaf of bread
Where rushing youths will push and kick:
My strength is like a woollen thread,
Weak are my legs and bent my head
I must not fall and break my hip
When climbing to my lonely bed:
Now that am old.

No Beauty Oil

Man's esteemed life, ensnared in sin,
Cannot reverse the curse within,
It falls to cancer and disease
Like rotting apples on the trees.

Should life be long, his skin will crease
Till he fulfils his rented lease;
His bones and joints may cry with pain
Or stroke destroys half of his brain.

No beauty oil or cleansing cream
Can hide her wrinkles when they scream;
The tints and colours for her hair
Are camouflage for what is there.

No medicine or purchased care
Halts the process of wear and tear,
The rich and wise, like fools may drool,
Disintegrate like skunk and mule.

All those in whose life Christ did reign
Will rise to be renewed again,
But the rebellious will be spewed
Into hell's torment unsubdued.

The Hotel

Standing by day, calling by night,
A great structure, a splendid sight,
A fortress filled with food and light.

Standing beside the open sea,
An awesome sight for all to see,
Inviting all, inviting me.

A storehouse, topped with food and drink,
With empty heads and some that think,
Who count the world their bath and sink.

The sound of mirth, squeal of laughter
Bounce from walls of painted plaster,
Made to outlast the hereafter.

When in building it caused to die
A stranger who worked to supply
Shelter and fun for rich and high.

Each time I have to pass the place
I see afresh that poor man's face
Crushed like a pear or wooden case.

His head was smashed - a building stone
Fell from a height and crushed each bone
Till it no longer looked his own.

His body was sent to his land,
His folk could never understand
Why his worth was an ounce of sand!

Angharad

Feeling like a mighty lord,
Pressing as a Moghul horde,
His foot hard against the floor,
Music like a great uproar,
He engaged the corner fast,
Screeching breaks could not hold fast:
The disaster was complete:
Overturning till his feet
Ended higher than his head
Which hit the windscreen and bled.

When he faced the sudden blow
He was sure his blood would flow,
That he would lose out on life
And face death's double-edged knife.
Now she would be left alone
To weep, remember and groan,
To earn her drink and her bread
And sleep in a lonely bed.
Knowing her life would be sad,
He yelled with pain, Angharad.

A driver upon that way
Stopped to see if he could sway
The outcome of this great crash:
Grasped his mobile in a flash
And he dialled nine nine nine,
Told them he would hold the line
To see if he could assist
With instructions which consist
Of first aid in what may seem
Hours till wailing sirens scream.

The ambulance and police came,
Searched his pockets for his name,
Broke the glass with a crowbar,
Pulled him out of the dead car
Which was like a ruined shack,
Like a cockroach on its back.
They laid him upon the ground,
Saw that his long bones were sound,
Rushed him to the nearest place
Famous as a trauma base.

The blood clot was then removed
From his head and he improved,
But remained in coma's sleep
While his vital signs did keep
Within the realm of a cure -
They hoped his brain would endure.
One day he opened his eyes
And to the nurse's surprise
He mumbled, then she heard
Her name, he called Angharad.

The Blind Child

(Based on an anonymous Arabic Poem)

Mother, what shape is the sky?
What is the moon or the light?
You speak of their great splendour
Which is obscured from my sight;
Is the world filled with darkness
Like the blackness that I see?
My mother, give me your hand
And do not go far from me.

I walk, but fear to stumble,
Alike the night as the day
With no guidance for my steps
Whether short or long the way;
I wonder, on my pathway,
Which may be rugged or plain
If I should meet with danger
And holes to trap me again.

My stick remains my eyesight,
But does it see with an eye?
Does it breathe, suffer and feel?
Does it listen when I cry?

The children play around me
Not knowing worry or fear
While I am blind and lonely
With their shouting in my ear;
It is God who observes me,
Keeps my steps lest I fall,
Shows me kindness in my life
When for His mercy I call.

The Lions

We came from a conquered nation to the
conqueror's domain
Almost twelve years after the war, sailing the
Channel again,
We saw, at the edge of the sea, the white cliffs in the rain.

We ventured into the cities where industry
keeps its heart,
Cities which played in our defeat a most
striking vital part
Where those who endured the furnace heat
were loyal from the start.

I looked upon the older folk with
amazement when I saw
That nothing in them inspired fear,
nothing generated awe,
Yet with firm determination they hammered
the fatal blow.

Women carrying shopping bags at the bus stops
where they queued
Seemed so innocent, made no fuss, yet they
had us barbecued;
I felt strongly that with great ease their sort
could have been subdued.

Turning to my friend I asked him to enlighten
and explain:
Are they the ones who won the war, who
caused our glory to wane?
Destroyed us on the battlefield, perhaps
could do it again?

How can it be that by their hand our noble
soldiers wee slain?
Theirs the lion which raised its head with
its blue and khaki mane?
The lion which stood in our land, upon the
Rhine and Main?

He answered, it is surely they who caused
our eagle to flee;
They have given the lion birth, the lion,
undaunted, free
Who roared within our Fatherland and
forced us to bend the knee.

Though it was severely wounded in its head,
heart and liver,
Although its blood dripped on our earth
into the soil and river,
It championed the cause of freedom, feared
not our loaded quiver.

The old lions had taught their young to be
magnanimous, bold,
To fight proudly for their domain, as being
of the same mould:
Consider the mighty lion when you look
upon the old.

The Flood

Look father, an added woe:
The water level is rising;
Where, oh where can we now go?
Is death fishing while disguising?
We covered one hundred miles
Fleeing swiftly before the foe;
Insecure, we lost out smiles,
Fear is the companion we know;

Hungry, tired, lame and unclean,
Hunted while life hurried away
Till this land of patchy green
Offered hope for a better day.
Father, the river rises,
It has also become our foe;
Death has many surprises,
To which corner can we go?

The Nile was swelled by the rain
Submerging its once peaceful bank
Flooding the green flat terrain
Till crops became sodden and sank.
Means of nurture were destroyed

In a fistful of numbered days:
The fruit of labour employed,
The ripening wheat and the maize.

Days passed slowly then death came
To snatch its victims from famine,
To bend men's skeletal frame
Not covered with cloth or linen;
Pot-bellies and sunken eyes,
Prominent bones and bulky knees
Were claimed for its special prize
While helpless beside barren trees.

Little sister, come with me
To life and safety in the north;
Let us turn our backs and flee,
Perhaps a new hope will spring forth;
Come, ride up upon my back
Although my own body is frail:
You will make a tiny pack
And good fortune may yet prevail.

She sat in a muddy place
Leaning against a dirty stone;
Flies picked at her little face;
It was easy to count each bone.
Death has not come through water:
A great mercy it would have been,
Famine champions the slaughter,
The dreadful master is too keen.
Water of life, raging deep:
Death's herald sent to the dying
Who on the thick mud they shall creep
Too weak for sighing or crying.

Shyness

Some rural aged people are shy
To almost being odd
For in their self-demeaning eye
Their doctor is a god.

I said to the farmer my friend,
How did your dear wife die?
"She did not seem ever to mend",
But he did not know why.

I said, I saw she grew too slim,
She lost a lot of weight.
He said, "the story is too grim:
Lost four stones down to eight".

Did her doctor explain to you
What was wrong with her chest?
He said, "he did not give one clue,
I think it was her breast".

And did you not venture to ask
The result of her scan?

"It would have been a heavy task:
        He is a famous man".

I know you asked when your prized cow
        Through sickness lost its life,
        But after you buried her now
        Know nothing of your wife.

Llyn Eiddwen

A minor road from the main road
Leads up Trefenter hill;
Despite the hard years' heavy load
I can remember still
The dreadful feeling and the mode
Which gave my spine a chill.

The angry sky was like a jar
Ready to drench the day;
The narrow road allowed one car
To hug the lane one way;
I edged aside upon the tar
Far from the ditch of clay.

As I, with caution moved up hill,
Two savage dogs appeared;
It seemed as if their bark could kill:
My heart trembled and feared;
They hugged the car with dogged will:
It could hardly be steered.

They were two sheep dogs, loyal, keen,
Their coat was black and white;
A rabid wolf could not have been
More vicious in my sight:
Saliva dripped from jaws too mean
And well prepared to bite.

I hoped the glass would keep them out
In my doubting concern;
I tried to change my way about:
There was no room to turn;
I had to creep past each moist snout
For I could not return.

They jumped the car, the front and rear,
And followed me awhile;
In normal times I would not fear:
Would look at them and smile,
But I felt as a hunted deer
Along this ten miles mile.

I passed an old lifeless dwelling
And came to rugged land
Where large rocks, proud and compelling,
Made a determined stand;
I moved forward, my pulse swelling
My clammy shaking hand.

As I climbed the barren hill
There was a downward trend:
The gentle curve of a fine quill
And not an acute bend;
Then I saw with an instant chill
That earth and sky did blend.

It was as if the ocean came
To spread beneath the sky;
I did not know "Llyn" was the name
For lake, however high;
I felt as one helpless, lame,
Ready to drown and die.

Llyn Eiddwen rests above the sea
And forms a splendid show,
But I was lost and dogs chased me,
Scared me from head to toe;
The lake should fill the heart with glee
As local farmers know.

The Welshman

His back was against the window,
The nearby mountain could be seen;
A green robe covered the meadow,
The mountain's was a satin sheen;
His head in the mountain's shadow
Was white before the peak had been.

Blind eyes fixed at me, yet twinkled:
A lighthouse, beckoned in the dark;
On features, though gaunt and wrinkled,
Firm resolve implanted its mark;
Experience of life had sprinkled
Its honour on a patriarch.

Sharp nose, an eagle's beak, sharp brain,
A powerful splendour soon showed
Mightier than the high terrain
On the day that the heavens snowed
Where the Dovey, swelled by the rain
Rushed down to the sea as it flowed.

He turned his ear and attended
To my words which were loud and slow;
Its deep caverns were defended
By bristles as white as the snow;
I saw how his mind depended
On knowledge he gained long ago.

He spoke wisely of distant lands,
Of affairs of peasant and king,
Of blades of grass and desert sands,
Of farming and of birds on wing;
I sat amazed between his hands:
Enjoyed the stories he did bring.

I sorely missed his departing:
Such men are sunken treasure, lost;
What quenches the flame of parting?
I recall his face at a cost
While daffodils keep on sprouting
To break on the hill through the frost.

Mam

For twenty years I watched her come
To the garden of the dead
With her two daughters beside her
And a scarf upon her head;
I saw her walk to a certain spot
In the shadow of sunset
To meditate, wait and ponder
Where the smooth black stone was set;
The showers of rain drops might fall
And sprinkle the grass blades wet,
But she would stand against the wind
Silent and most loyal yet;
I vouch that her deep tenderness
Is the deepest I have met.

Standing motionless at the grave
With a daughter at each arm,
Thinking of loved ones now sleeping
Away from the gates of harm;
Thinking of days gone forever,
Generous with joy and charm.

Not once did she carry flowers
Or bring roses in her hand:
She was lovelier than a rose
And exceedingly more grand;
Her very presence in the place
Added beauty to the land.

She brought her many memories
To her husband and daughter;
The child was run down by a car
Whose driver did the slaughter;
She was purer than any pearl
Or lily in the water.

She visited them with anguish,
With a heart broken and torn
But could never lament aloud
Although she wept when alone;
The cuckoo cried out in the wood
The sad cry of one forlorn;
Her little girl was her cuckoo
From the day that she was born.

She chose the biblical statement
Upon the polished head stone:
Words of longing, of aching love
Which cried, "Until the day dawn".
I watched when she was bent and old
Needing her girls for support,
Looking hopefully for the morn
When death will bring comfort.
In that Welsh valley and churchyard
The bleating of the sheep
Breaks the silence of the still air

Where in the grave she will sleep,
Three together, patient until
Each rises with radiant face,
But in the meanwhile God looks on
And watches their resting place.

The Hill

I wondered if a poisoned dart
Or a lover's sharp-pointed knife
Once lodged firmly in his young heart,
Kept him unmarried all his life.

Pale and sweating, it was his time
To journey to another land,
His lungs were moist and full of slime,
His legs could not hold him to stand.

He asked for me as nightfall crept
To testify with his last breath,
To tell the secret which he kept
Of how he was cheated by death.

"It was beneath the cedar tree
One evening in the fading light
When I felt she was part of me,
Esteemed her more than my eyesight.

I took her hand and asked her why
She will never regret nor rue

That of God's men it should be I
Who gained her love, buoyant and true?

She led me up upon the hill
And said she found my heart was pure
And in the twilight, clear and still,
She held me tight till I was sure.

The days rushed like a morning dream
And seemed to fly on buzzard's wings
When death snatched her while in midstream
And cut her like a knot of strings."

Then with a voice both strong and staid
Before his mind began to stray
He begged of me and almost prayed
To grant his favoured piece of clay.

"She held me captive to her charms
Where I did pledge my soul and will;
There she embraced me with her arms:
Bury my body on that hill."

Famine

Let not the sun rise in the east,
Nor let the dough ferment with yeast
When some men starve while others feast,
The poor more wretched than the beast.

His belly swells for want of food
While greedy men delight to brood
On flavours which their mouths subdued,
But he ate dirt and bit and chewed.

One with the earth, one with the dust,
His hope is lost, he stinks like must;
Earth's bosom is a lifeless crust:
Dry and wrinkled, a shrivelled bust.

His wasted tears no longer flow:
Their fountains ceased three moons ago;
Sinews melted like summer's snow;
Beneath loose skin his bare bones show.

The mother who travailed and gave
Life to a child she cannot save

Sees those dim eyes hide in a cave
Then hugs the earth, her bed and grave.

While men perish like desert flies,
Food is burned that prices may rise;
Earth produces bounteous supplies:
The rich man feeds, the poor man dies.

Some bless the day that they were born,
Others wish they remained unborn:
In famine's jaws, mangled and torn,
Hoping that death precedes the morn.

Lord, injustice reigns in the land:
Some men, like mighty fir trees, stand,
Their fellows perish like firebrand,
Their food the air, the dust, the sand.

Africa

Those walking skeletons covered with skin,
Exposed in all parts with sores on the shin
Are too young for hair to grow on their chin,
Too lean for death: it snatches hundreds in.

Squatting skeletons upon the dry ground,
Motionless and silent without a sound,
Oblivious that burial pits are found,
Cluttered with corpses till their turn comes round.

Exhausted skeletons show no surprise
When their mouths and noses are covered with flies
That suck the moisture from these and their eyes
As they lay helpless, unable to rise.

We watch them on the television screen
Between food adverts, which seems too obscene,
With no other record that they have been
A part of this world, stuck in a latrine.

The nations supplied food and drugs to heal,
But bellies swelled for the lack of a meal

When warring scoundrels continued to steal
And mercy died in hearts moulded of steel.

O Lord, speed the time when justice prevails
That food may reach camps, villages and vales,
The land of the vacant mouth and entrails
Where the weak cannot cry when death assails.

Not Tonight

Leaving the womb, a moonless night,
We take a breath and cry with might,
Howling as we first meet the light
Like battling men with death in sight.

We flourish and increase in height,
Life throbs in veins, the world is bright,
Our souls forbid evil to blight
The will to live, however slight.

The sunset years precede the night:
Age comes with pain to wound and bite,
As death draws near we cry with fright:
Not yet, not yet, no, not tonight.

As You Lay Dying

Cyclamen covers the fields with white,
Poppies sprinkle its dress with red,
Spring's nature displays a splendid sight
As you lay dying on your bed.

The field owl rehearsed its song last night,
Blackbirds try to match it today;
All creatures rejoice to meet the light
And you are struggling just to stay.

The eagle glides in majestic flight,
It eyes searching for its prey;
Nature portrays cruelty with might,
Against our will takes you away.

You abandon me in my sore plight
To face alone the world's decay;
I will languish, but struggle to fight
Until I follow you one day.

He Kissed My Hand

He stood before me, a tall dark man, strong and true,
Son of the open desert where he lived and grew,
Robed with white majesty, yet with uncovered head
Came to ask if his father was alive or dead.

The old man had wandered upon the wide expanse
Where the beams of sunlight flirted in a strange dance;
As he crossed the highway, his feet weary and sore,
A car rushed him like a bull to crush him and gore.

His right limbs were broken and blood dripped
from his side;
His skull was fractured causing a haemorrhage inside;
Some bleeding from a wounding occurred in his brain
And there was a major hole in a surface vein.

There was no time to meddle; there was no time to wait:
A delay in treatment would quickly seal his fate:
His brain, firmly compressed by a blood clot that formed
Would buckle beneath its force and become deformed.

The urgent operation was done with great haste:
It was the only way to redeem him from waste,
But his natural days will run their plotted course
Until God who gave him life takes it to its source.

His son came to thank me that his father was spared;
I gave him my hand to shake; he looked hard and stared,
Then he took it to his lips, kissed my hand and bowed;
I felt small and embarrassed while he sobbed aloud.

The Pigeon

I like to travel in the night
And at the break of day
To make up time by speedy flight
Bur for one thing I pray
That creatures dazzled by my light
May not run in my way.

I dread to kill the bird and hare,
The rabbit and the hog;
Such creatures, delightful and fair,
Are safer by the bog,
But in the cool fresh morning air
May wander in the fog.

The apple trees were in new bud
Adorning the roadside,
While pigeons searched around the mud
For food on the wayside;
One struck my windscreen with a thud:
I think it must have died.

It hurt my soul that I had slain
A young frightened wild fowl.
It left no smudge or fresh bloodstain
But I uttered a howl.
I wished it had a sharper brain
Like that of a barn owl.

Lost at Sea

The men have returned from their fishing and toil
Heading for the land standing grey in the sun
Longing for their homes, for their wives, for their soil,
Their journey seemed endless, a turbulent one.

The dwellers in the hamlet run to the shore,
Counting the approaching sails, all glittering white,
Their hearts bursting with the fear and joy they store
As they glimpse their brave men coming into sight.

They hug their women and their children draw near
But standing alone, she stares upon each wave,
Where is my husband? she cries with frenzied fear,
Has he been buried in a watery grave?

They placed his new fishing gear upon the sand,
His yellow coat, with his tackle and his net:
Hold me in my sorrow, I can hardly stand:
Heartbreak is my path that woe has paved and set.

"Young woman, you must find it hard to believe
That the raging waves embraced his youthful life.

What comfort can we give? But you can retrieve
The memories of his youth with you, his wife.

Ask the cruel sea that seems so peaceful now,
Ask the silent men who saw him slip and fall,
Who saw the water submerge his handsome brow,
How he cried out your name in his final call."

The Cliff

The cliff has watched the ages, watched them come and go,
It saw the men of valour stand against the foe;
It watched invading armies rush against the coast:
Hard men prepared for battle who made death their boast.

At times it watched the seamen on seas high and calm
Working at the break of day with a tender charm
But sweating for a living in the vast expanse
With souls exposed to danger where the high waves dance.

It oft looked on the children running on the beach,
It watched their joyful playing by their guardians' reach,
The life of all seemed carefree, full of fun and joy,
Saw the baby cuddled warm grow into a boy.

It heard the billows raging in the depth of night,
The wind beating the waters with ferocious might
While in the storms of winter, snow and sea did meet
Until they were united in a kiss of sleet.

It heard the cry of seagulls wailing through the air
Calling in the morning mist for their young to stir;

It saw the glorious sunset burn the sea and sky,
Glowing with a fiery flame that was soon to die.

But now it hears you sobbing, preparing to jump,
To discard your precious life like a rotten stump.
Peace will find you tomorrow, live in hope today,
God will comfort your sorrow, guide you on your way.

Ruby

You were agile and bouncing with vigour,
Laughter most heartily moving your soul,
Nothing was hard for you to endeavour,
Life came to find of your beauty its goal.

How did that illness fall hard upon you?
How did it strike at the cells of the nerve?
Tongue and vocal chords failed to obey you
When once they proclaimed your glorious verve.

Your mind prevailed but suffered with sadness,
It saw that weakness grabbed you and assailed;
Only your strength prevented the madness
From tearing your soul, though it tried and failed.

You bore it in silence, did not wallow
In pity though life was hideously hard
Until at the end you could not swallow
Nor breathe as your wasted muscles were marred.

True faith in the Christ was your security,
Kept you sane as paralysis did creep,

Ruby, you were a gem of purity
Though now in the grave you restfully sleep.

For years I have missed you nor seen your face,
For years I have sorrowed with you in pain
But our great Saviour has prepared your place:
We shall be together, alive again.

The Vultures

Stand patiently, quietly by,
Hear the buzzards of heaven cry:
They rapidly glanced their food.
Let them glide gracefully and fly
Until they alight from the sky
To devour a life subdued.

Upon leafless branches perching,
Their open eagle eyes searching
For signals of a life's end.
Vultures gather for meat and bread
To pluck the remains of the dead
With stout beaks which tear and rend.

Covetous men wait for the old,
Praying that death, dreadful and cold,
Will cause them to wilt and sag.
It will be time to claim their lot,
To fill their belly and fleshpot
And use their riches to brag.

Wearing hypocrisy's false mask,
Devotion is their easy task
To guard their kinsman's treasure.
The worm of gain, a gnawing pest,
Forbids the use of money lest
The estate drops by measure.

A silent partner has his share,
Will value the house, bed and chair,
The cattle, the land, the hut.
The taxman will not fail to come
To review and work out the sum
And gather his legal cut.

Life's hurricane travels man's way,
It may uproot and tear away
His life of pitiful greed.
Young men often lie in the grave,
Cowards may fall before the brave
And worms waken to feed.

Mother

Alas, they took you to a foreign land
Leaving my father buried in the sand:
You were too ill to know or understand
When a kind nation held you by the hand.

Amidst the fire and blundering outrage,
Amidst the terror, turbulence and rage,
You found yourself within a closing cage
Having to flee in your advancing age.

Man's body grows old, creases and decays
Through hardship, illness, weariness of days;
The spirit matures until it portrays
The soul's true nature in its basic ways.

You fled when young, you fled when you were old
Although your young heart was robust and bold;
You had six children to guard and uphold:
A common story, now often retold.

Twice a refugee, no town of your own,
A fragrant jasmine, then planted, now blown

By human hands which cut you to the bone,
   Yet were not heard to cry or ever moan.

A calm widow of twenty years or more
   Who kept my father's memory in store
That many thought you had no bleeding sore:
   Your feelings rushed like waves toward the shore.

At last, you lived far from your husband's grave –
Where you should have slept, for which you did crave –
   And there you died, patient and pure and brave,
   Not hoarding hatred: you truly forgave.

You died, your noble spirit did not die:
   The spirit does not age or close its eye;
You went to be with your Saviour on high:
   No home on earth, a mansion in the sky.

Life

The echo of a wailing voice, returned by the hills,
Answers the agony of soul when death strikes and kills,
Until the mind cannot forget its torments and ills.

Fountains emerging from red eyes gushed upon the ground
Like sorely weeping summer skies where
monsoons abound,
Will the merciless hand of time heal a wound unbound?

Will salty water from sad eyes join rivers that flow
Across the plains and rocky land, reeling as they go?
Or will the longing of the heart ride the sea of woe?

The proud mother enjoys her child for a little while
Then sprinkles soil on his box when life
proceeds with guile,
His face is gone, his shout, his call, his laugh,
play and smile.

The bride, wondrous in appearance on her wedding day,
Wails upon her husband's corpse, soon to join the clay,

None can procure balm or hope when
death collects its pay.

Children bury their own parents, feeling biting grief;
The earth has taken to stealing: has become a thief;
Corruption turns beauty to dust while man's life is brief.

Human life is a worthless game if for aye we die
And is the greatest mockery underneath the sky
If we should perish forever with a final sigh.

If man's spirit does not endure when his days have run,
How hopeless then his destiny since time had begun:
The dead soared to eternity, to meet God, each one.

Dusk

Doctor, please save my husband's life:
He is the whole of life to me;
If left alone to face the strife
My spirit will cower and flee.

My soul's support for many years
In sadness and joy all sharing;
I see the sword that cuts and sears
To remove from me his caring.

But this apart, I love him so
With all my powers perceiving
That he must not suffer and go
Not say, farewell, I am leaving.

I cherish the touch of his hand,
His strong eyes to look into mine
Before his life loses its strand,
His great spirit its crumbling shrine.

O Lord, hear my prayer this day,
Remember to welcome and greet
My love at the end of the way
That leads to Your heavenly seat.

Burial

In mildewed room, on open shelf, his body, silent, bare,
Lay cold, alone and motionless in cool and musty air
While once bright eyes, now glazed and soft, looked at
nothing, nowhere.

Disconcerted as a bird, its young dead on the coast
With breaking heart my wet eyes saw the man I
loved the most:
Could I behold the face of death and still make
life my boast?

To clothe him was no easy task with limbs stiff as a block;
A man, once mighty, was like wood and I am of his stock;
When blood oozed from a puncture site it
gave me quite a shock.

My mother wailed in church aloud while
staring at his head;
My sister wept with tears that flowed from
sparkling eyes turned red;
Others gathered to see the show: put on the lid, I said.

His final journey on this earth was in a wooden chest;
The red crescent guided the cars which
journeyed to the west
Till we reached the burial ground where we
laid him to rest.

When I returned after a time, my mother at my side,
I saw the desert sun had worked to let the grave subside.
My memories will haunt that place
Where he still sleeps outside.

The Day of My Mother's Travail

They said, "come, let us celebrate
The day when you were born,
When you squeezed through the narrow gate
Into the light of morn."

They told me that I howled and cried
Like barbarians at war
When my mother pushed me outside
Out of the exit door.

I was as slimy as a snail:
Wrinkled skin and visage,
They placed me in a metal scale
And weighed me like cabbage.

They said that day, "a boy, a male!
May long life be his gain"
But it was my mother's travail,
A day or cries of pain

The Man

I saw him on the pavement in the crowded street
As I was returning home on my aching feet,
The sad grimace of his face said that he would weep
For within his eyes there was sorrow lying deep.

He carried a sturdy stick to open his way,
To steady his gait and keep rushing men at bay;
His lips were parted and limp as he looked ahead,
His suit was neat and he wore a hat upon his head.

Compassion flared within me at his anguished face,
I could not halt a stranger or reduce his pace;
How lonely can a man be in a busy crowd
Where their commotion and noise rises high and loud.

Whether in the borough street or Parliament Square
One stands alone in the world with no one to care,
Despite the milling of the throng rushing around
One can be as in his room or in empty ground.

At Twilight

When night descends upon city and field
My eyelids close melodiously to yield
To the arms of sleep, caressed by its hand
As darkness robes the splendour of the land,
Then in my twilight moments I recall
The scenes of life, the triumph and the fall,
The powerful who live a life most fair,
The miserable, in fear and despair,
The poor, disgraced before men's cruel eyes,
The proud, thriving on treachery and lies.

I recall the meek, tossed like tennis balls,
Unjustly confined within prison walls,
The rowdy free, unmoved by ill or word,
Held by sensuous smiles, by whispers heard.
The old, on the whole, are not full of days,
The young may not see the end of their ways:
The pitfalls abound for the youthful feet
Who presume to face all the traps they meet
Along the paths that lead to drugs and pain,
To death which waits within alley and lane
Until their soul is like a finger, lost

In heat of battle or Antarctic frost.
When the sun rises to deport the night
They cannot abide the pure morning light
But lie in dungeons where darkness prevails
Far from the mountains, the green field and dales.

I clearly see that life's journey is short
Though most will refuse to leave it and will snort
When their hour draws near to the hungry grave:
The cowards are many, few are the brave.

There is beyond time a Heaven made sure
For all who honour God, the blessed poor,
But a place remains, dreadful to behold
For those who remain in the devil's hold.

Money

He left England one winter's night
To where the sun is warm and bright
To make a living in the land
Where oil is found in sea and sand.
His future seemed good and secure
Though he found it hard to endure
The harsh weather, the fiery sun
Making life hard for everyone.
Air conditioning helped him bear
The blasting heat and humid air;
His skilful work filled up his days
And all the natives gave him praise.
His little children could be taught
Better than in England, he thought:
When they grow up he will then go
Though riches will shout at him, NO!
They must not enter boarding school
Where teachers will usurp his rule,
But first he will make a packet
From this money making racket.
In time he said, next year I leave

But in his heart did not believe
That he will lay his wealth aside
And then in England will abide.
Thousands of pounds lived in his soul
Till it became a great black hole;
His children went to boarding school:
He lost their love, became a fool.
I leave next year, again he said
But he laid still in the same bed.
He said, I shall retire quite soon:
The stars waxed and waned with the moon
And in a foreign land he stayed,
His conscience could not be obeyed.
When I return I put at stake
My wealth which the tax man will take:
Let me find a land in a while
Where I can be a tax exile.
The ruler has become the slave,
Money the master, he the knave.

Innocence

There lived a lovely little girl
In Cymmer by Maesteg
Where two sweet shops were filled with pearls
Beside the chapel gate.
Now Mrs. Havard's door was shut
With handle set too high
For such a small child who could not
Reach it although she tried.
Across the street was Wilf John's shop
With door slightly ajar,
She looked then ran and made one hop
Just like a shooting star.
The innocence of childhood's child
Did not know guile or flare:
She stood inside, gentle and mild
Without worry or care.
Sweets were sold by Wilf John, she said
Wilf John, come, cross the street,
Come, open Mrs. Havard's door,
I want to buy some sweets.
I give you Mrs. Havard, he said
And stamped hard with his feet.

Night Take-Off

It was only a single hour since our parting goodbye,
Since she went to board the jet plane waiting its turn to fly.
A bright red light winked in its head as if it meant to say,
We are ready to be airborne, to travel on our way.
The elephant trunk was lifted before they shut the gates,
Before the giant was shifted as if it rolled on skates.
Falcon crested, saw the tarmac to which it slowly crept,
Eager to cross the continents while weary people slept.
It headed toward the runway at a leisurely speed
With colours flashing at variance, warning
men to take heed.
It stopped like a champion sprinter who fills
his lungs with air
Then it charged with a mighty roar of a beast in a snare.
It lifted its experienced nose, sniffed the heavens and smelt
Then ascended toward the sky, to where
the darkness dwelt.
It flew to join the distant stars in the vast silent deep,
The thick silence that it shattered by
engines roused from sleep.
The hair stood straight upon my skin when
I saw her depart,

My moistened eyes could not put out the
burning of my heart.

The Aeroplane

O silver Bird, flying across the sky,
Flying higher than any bird can fly,
Watching the clouded earth as you pass by,
The blue ocean, and mountains standing high;
You caused hearts to weep with sorrow and sigh,
You took away loved ones who once were nigh,
They cried with glaring eyes and said goodbye;
Some could not know peace, others wondered why?
Many knew in a moment they would die
While loved ones remained to lament and cry.

Flying high like a mighty giant bird,
No flap of your wings or calls can be heard,
Just noise to drown the cries of those who cared,
Those who remember all the love they shared.

Above the lightning with its dazzling glare,
Through roaring storms which trouble hearts and scare,
Through many airy pits, many a snare
You travel to distant lands, anywhere,
No bird can dare to do the things you dare:
You are the master of the sky and air.

Your bowels carry business men and boys,
Women, and girls with all their varied toys
Whose hearts are proud to mingle with your joys,
But in some souls a dreadful fear annoys
That you will fail, though the captain employs
His mind and skill to safeguard your alloys
Lest you carry all from this world of noise.

Return, O Bird, from distant lands, return,
The hearts remains restless, ready to burn
Until are seen your mighty wings and stern,
Are seen by those who from your journeys learn
That life is fickle, yet for life they yearn.
Return, silver bird, be a shining star,
Bring to me my love, bring her from afar.

Conflict

National Anthem

My country, blessed be your name:
From you both truth and justice came
To the nations of mankind.
Sun of the morning, brightest sun,
Heaven weaved your landscape and spun:
Earth home of our God, the Son.

My fathers' land from ages past,
Home of the wanderer, the outcast,
A priceless treasure to find.
Until time dies you shall remain
The queen of lands, beauty's domain
While nations flourish and wane.

Freedom's banner rippled on high,
Wisdom descended from the sky
When darkness engulfed the mind;
Your infants learnt to honour life
While elsewhere, barbarism was rife,
Paganism, bloodshed and strife.

Mother of truth, beacon of light,
Disperse your foes of wrong and night,
Release the prisoner, the blind;
Call your scattered, your poor, your lame,
Heal their wounds and give them the flame
To extend your worthy fame.

My homeland, I rise up and swear
To guard your soil and sea and air
Against the morally blind.
My heart's loud praises shall resound,
I tread with care your holy ground
Where your martyred sons are bound.

Despair

I said, come let us drink the wine together
From the early night until the newborn morn;
Strengthen a weak heart, broken as a feather,
By the hardness of life, buffeted and torn.

Do not leave me in the night of my sorrow,
Come into my heart and pluck from it the pain,
Let solace remain till the waiting morrow,
Let me forget that death is hunting again.

Save me from the mercy of merciless men
As they delight to crush and destroy my soul;
Stand with me as loyally as you did when
The great billows raged and threw me to the wall.

Should accidents break me and batter my head,
Should boulders and nails engulf and wound my feet,
It would not compare with the small piece of lead
Which sends a man to eternity, dead as meat.

My land is ravaged from within and without,
The land of my ancestors from ages past;
I hear its cry of pain, its loud bitter shout
As tyranny makes its poor children outcast.

Its meadows unite with pure crystal rivers
Of water which gives life to the fertile soil
Yet it suffers while my crying soul shivers
For its men scattered like manure in the spoil.

The eagle roosts safely in the mountain top
Far from the guns which burn and shatter and slay
But the warring parties still refuse to stop
Their slaughter of innocents each passing day.

My brothers hold weapons of powder and steel
To save the land is their united desire,
To make the enemy fall, retreat and reel:
Their homeland in their hearts, in their hands the fire.

They defy destruction, though savage and sour;
The earth receives their outpoured water of life;
The sky, like a volcano of great power,
Sends them to their death, ending their noble strife.

Come and share with me the bitterness of fate
From the early night until the newborn morn,
Perhaps hope and life will yet regenerate:
Will my homeland be free? Will it yet be reborn?

Uprooted

They did not think or even know
That men will force them all to go
Far from their ancient land of birth
To distant corners of the earth.

As babes upon their mother's breast
They found within her arms a rest
While she watched in their wakeful eyes
The splendid moon, the starry skies.

As infants growing without care
Heedless of gun-smoke in the air
Were startled by the canon's sound,
The noise of bullets flung around.

They fled in sorrow with no fun
Knowing full well they had to run
Before the shearer came to wield
His shears on rosebuds in the field.

And now he lives upon their land
Which he obtained with bloodied hand
Forever fearful that the sword
Will cut him like a dying gourd.

Their homeland cried when it was raped,
With open jaws they looked and gaped
And now with enemies is draped:
Its holy soil and its seascape.

The Land Cries

Why do you kill my children?
Why do you spill their blood?
I bore them on my bosom
I see their tearful flood,
I hear their shout of anguish,
Lament their fearful cry,
I feel them drop in my lap
As they fall down and die.

Have mercy on my children,
Why should they meet their fate?
Why should a bullet slay them
And death grasp them as bait?
They have not fully grown up,
They are still young, though brave,
Pluck not the tender rosebuds
Nor send them to their grave.

They rise up to defend me
With all their strength and breath;
Why do make them suffer

To kiss the hand of death?
Do spare my little children,
Just let them grow and live;
You will then learn how quickly
They will not take, but give.

The Comforter

Say not your years were spent in vain
Wasted and fruitless from the start;
Let not your spirit die in pain
Wounded and stricken with a dart;
Though our sons were savagely slain
Their country knows they did their part;
Each lion fell with coloured mane
Drenched by the blood from its own heart
Which emptied out its crimson stain
To feed the topsoil of the main.

Think of their spirit yet again
From whose essence honour did flow,
Of their homeland's mountain and plain
That called their sons to rise and go,
Clad with courage to bear the strain
And stand steadfast against the foe;
To free the land was their refrain
That all may live in peace and grow;
They sneered at death with proud disdain
Exchanged their lives for their domain.

We taught them early to sustain
Hardship with fortitude each day;
Their names will shine and never wane
As years roll slowly in decay;
Young children will learn to retain
And tell their story by the way.
But come to my heart, there remain
Never to leave, ever to stay;
My shameless eyes fail to restrain
My tears which pour down like the rain.

Oppression

Shake the mountain, break the fountain,
Fill the sea with sand,
Explode the sun, cause men to run,
Give us back our land,
Let the sky birds, the cattle herds
On its meadows stand.

Let the green vine give grapes for wine,
Let our people live,
Let each star in heaven afar
Its faint twinkle give,
Dispel the clouds, remove the shrouds,
We will then forgive.

Remove the chain, the crushing pain
From our aching heart,
Let us again bless heaven's rain,
Give us a fresh start,
We will then toil upon our soil,
Of heaven a part.

Let the brown root spring forth a shoot,
Life again will bloom,
Cause our mind its peace to find,
Cut the bonds of doom,
Come all free sons, throw down your guns,
Just think, there is room.

The Oppressed

Oh, bitterness, is there no end?
Will heaven cleave, mercy descend?
The body withers with the soul
While tyrants kick them like a ball.

Rising awhile, again to fall,
Danger without, within the gall;
Only their blood will satisfy
Disdainful men deaf to their cry.

And some remain, they shall not die
Though raging men and hell reply;
The seed, though crushed, will grow again
Until new life will fill the plain.

The summer heat, the winter rain
Will bless the furrows bearing grain;
When seasons have tarried and run
The stem will shoot towards the sun.

The tempest raged, then it was gone:
Men and their houses fell as one;
The newborn crying out of sight
Carries the nation's life tonight.

Injustice

Say, Injustice, when were you born?
When did your eyes first see the morn?
You seems each say to be reborn!

Since your first parents went astray,
Since they departed from God's way
I am reborn anew each day.

Tell, Injustice, where do you live?
You seem all creatures to outlive:
Bloodshed and theft are gifts you give.

I live where man chooses to be,
I read his open heart and see
That sin makes him no longer free.

What are the deeds you like to do
Which none seems able to undo,
When men receive wages from you?

I place the just behind barbed wire,
Do the wicked man's desire,
Consume the poor with flames of fire.

Men heed me and slay each other,
They crush human rights and smother,
I set brother against brother.

I cause people to die in pain,
Destroy produce in field and plain,
Close ears to the cry of the slain.

I send the innocent to death,
Rob him of life as if by stealth
And fan his pyre by his own breath.

I beat men, give them their gruel,
Afflict them by means most cruel
Using Freedom's sons for fuel.

No class or kind escapes my hand,
They may face me as one strong band,
Yet on their necks is where I stand.

I catch the unborn in my net
Whose parents refuse to beget:
Would rather play and then forget.

I urge a man to leave his wife,
Rob her of youth then bare his knife,
Count her the mistake of his life.

Injustice, how else are you called?
I remember that I was told
Your name brings terror to the bold.

Oppression is my other name
Through which I earned my vaunted fame
To strike while others take the blame.

Injustice, have you many sons?
Were they nurtured on bread, or guns?
The brave flees their fury and runs.

My firstborn twins are my delight:
Their work brings pleasure to my sight
Though they try to regain the right.

They take my weapons and employ
My skill which they learnt to deploy
To hunt the guilty and destroy.

Vengeance, and Hatred, is each name;
Man's torment is their chiefest game
Till he asks not from where it came.

What constitutes your greatest deed
On which your soul must live and feed?
Is it adultery or greed?

My deeds are many, full of lust,
The one I must do, yes I must
Is to accuse and slay the just.

A gambler may lose then regain,
The shackled may sever his chain,
But life once lost, lives not again.

Injustice, begone into hell;
Let Justice flourish and do well;
May you never buy men and sell.

The Refugee

Living in a land where love is cold,
Where mercy is dead, oppression bold,
Where freedom cannot gain a firm hold.

His skin is wrinkled, his body old,
He yearns for the place where it was told
A newborn child has arrived, behold.

The dagger of time has marked his face,
His life was hunted from place to place:
His death a shame on the human race.

His hair, white as the Winter snows
Commands respect while dignity glows
To hide the sadness which no one knows.

Eyebrows like hills of bracken and slate
Arabian swords, crescent shaped and great
Await with patience the hand of fate.

His years fulfilled three scores and ten
Amidst a nation of lukewarm men
Until the end comes, but who knows when?

His thoughts attempt to capture the sound
Of boyhood seasons spent on the ground
Of his hometown where joy did abound.

The soul of man cannot cease to cry
To return to its birthplace and fly
That there it may live and there to die.

Alas, he must lie where his last breath
Leaves his body at the time of death
Far from the land of Megadeath.

His soul will acquire its long sought rest
When no one can harm it or molest:
Will friends and family call him blest?

The Rape of Kuwait - August 1990

Great tanks came rolling down the street,
The chains crackled, the road buckled,
Men fell like harvest grain of wheat;
Infants and babies who suckled
Were blown till they were chunks of meat,
Men and women, killed or shackled
Were harassed by the armoured fleet,
While young soldiers laughed and chuckled
Treading them down with their strong feet.

High heaven heard and sorely wept,
Shedding its tears, black as the night;
A woman wailed her son who slept
The sleep of death before her sight
Beneath the spreading jet-black cloud
Of smoke-filled sky, the burning suns
Of oil wells in the land once proud
Whose men have fallen to the guns,
Where slaughter, robbery were fun
Possessions carried by the ton.

The wealthy, peaceful Gulf once gave
Fish in abundance, wheat and oil,
Was turned into an open grave
Of birds and fish held in its soil.
Once seamen sailed the waves of light,
Made viscid with petroleum, black,
Where open sea and shoreline bight
Were filled with dead creatures and wrack.
Corruption in the earth was done
While flames threatened to burn the sky;
Rare darkness overwhelmed the sun
Where men were seized and held to die.
The helpless in their motherland
Perished by the assassin's hand.

Freedom

Look how he creeps on hands and knees
Pulling hard at the binding strap,
An infants knows not what he sees
Will free himself of bonds that trap.

It hatches in the nest and sings,
Is kept from the predator's mouth,
The fledgeling learns to beat its wings:
Propellers that will take it south.

Floating across the dark grey sky
The cloud bestows water and shade,
Moving to where the eagles fly
Freely across valley and glade.

Creatures reject bondage, capture,
Insects and fish, mammals and birds,
Freedom is their right by nature,
The prairie fox, the cattle herds.

God's gift given to all mankind
Yet not enjoyed by all who can;
Some are compelled to dig and grind
While kept in chains by fellow man.

Why are thousands held in cages
Forbidden the green hills and sea?
Despair rules, the mind engages
Hope that they may one day be free.

The baby breaths free air at birth,
Shares the freedom for which men crave
While evil villains of the earth
Enslave the weak until the grave.

Rise, living flame within the poor,
Buffeted on the rocks and stones,
No mortal can kill or obscure
Your fire within your children's bones.

Dying today, born tomorrow
Hanged unjustly and bound in shame
Yet from the graveyard of sorrow
Your sons will rise to bear your name.

Desire of all, owned by the few,
You heed the cries of those who call,
Oppressors never thought or knew
That your sons will secure their fall.

Some lived in dungeons of the night,
Some had to run to save their skin,
But will stand strong to gain their right
And prove that courage is their twin.

Invasion of Kuwait - August 1990

Father,
Did you hear the engines roaring?
Did you see the soldiers pouring
And their noisy rockets soaring
Down the street, past your feet?

Did you feel the earth was shaking?
Did you think the ground was breaking?
Did you hear the dead bones quaking
As if being reclothed with meat?

Did you see the oil wells burning?
Blue waters to blackness turning?
And the deep sea billows churning
The slurping oil slick passing by?

Did you see the seagulls drowning?
Cormorant and white tern browning

And gigantic thick flames crowning
The land and covering the sky?

Did you hear the great guns speaking?
Dusty chained metal wheels squeaking?
Did you see water drums leaking
And fighter planes screaming on high?

Were your dry bones, ready, restless
As men proud heads fell down senseless?
Father, you have heard the helpless,
Wait until the last trumpet's cry.

It is the time of oppression,
For men to practice transgression,
To take another's possession.
It is not Resurrection Day.

The neighbour with rude obsession
Proclaimed God in his confession
Then invaded with aggression
To ravage, rape and to inveigh.

The tanks rolled in, the guns were manned,
Destruction reigned, almost offhand,
No one was able to withstand
Those who entered to rob and slay.

There, in the heart of the city,
Mercy perished as did pity,
Squashed by boots, studied and gritty
Where carefree children used to play.

Your wife, a widow was ailing
As her health and strength were failing
While the soldiers were assailing
The homes of their innocent prey.

She should be with you when she dies,
When death comes in to close her eyes,
Her place stays vacant till you rise:
She will sleep in a different clay.

Friends moved her to a new domain
While daily fresh blood from the slain
Drenched the soldiers who killed like Cain,
Too weak to plead, she went away.

They left you in the ground alone
Lying beneath a marble stone
Which truly is a safer zone
Until the Resurrection Day.

Alfred

He was my brother in the Lord
Who felt Hitler's unholy sword.
He said, bury me when I die,
Let not the sparks lick me and fry,
But place me deep within the ground,
Burn me not with a sizzling sound:
The sad fate of my family
Who felt the burning bodily
As sinews melted from the bone
In the furnace where they were thrown.
Mother, you faced them without hope
When they transformed your fat to soap.
Have they not seen, you purified
Their stinking flesh, though putrified?
There is no hell, the foolish say,
Hell sees their deeds and runs away.

I was born a Bavarian Jew,
But who could tell that we would rue
That we belonged to such a land
Where human devils were to stand?

They baked us in the heated fire
As building bricks for their empire.
Can I forget them as they dragged
My mother while they laughed and bragged?
But pastor Franck saved from hell
When at Christ's feet I humbly fell.
I know I shall never return
To where men used to hunt and spurn.
Now I am old, ready to die,
To see my Saviour in the sky;
Cremation was my kindreds' fate,
Let me enter death's earthen gate,
Let my body be interred,
But let me not be scorched and burned.

Nature

First Light

While darkness covers dark and green
And night creatures frolic unseen,
When sleeping men begin to toss
And frogs jump high amidst the moss,
The night prepares to flee from sight
Like clouds that vanish in the night,
Like a whiff of smoke, blown away
To make room for another day.

Creeping on tiptoes in the dark,
Calling sparrow, robin, and lark
The light stretches its neck headlong
To be greeted by chirping song;
It enters slowly from beyond,
Uncovers mountain plain, and pond;
The darkness runs, it leaves no mark
While waking dogs begin to bark.

Sunset

Billions, billions tiny atoms
Join in pairs and explode
To scatter to man a blessing
Wherever his abode;
Though awesome in wildest fury
Man's heart does not forebode:
The hydrogen atoms fusing
Upon high heaven's road,
Are subject to the Almighty
Whose hands bind and encode
The great atom's finite power,
Its energy and mode.

The star, one of a myriad stars,
Runs swiftly to the west,
Leaving the lazy eastern shore,
Calling for men to rest,
Exposing its fiery body,
With naked, shining breast
To plunge into the water's depth
With urgent speed and zest;

Birds vainly follow where it sleeps
To build themselves a nest.

As if the seaman's hand can reach
To touch the ball of fire
Falling into the ocean's mouth
Out of the deep sapphire;
No sizzling is heard, no steam seen,
No waves rising higher;
The sea grows cold, should it not boil
To brig forth blood and mire
When the horizon is crimson
Like a flaming brier?

The creatures of the night awake,
To them the day is born.
In many souls a fire is lit
With memories reborn,
While others in darkness cower,
In loneliness to mourn,
Awaiting anxiously the light
To usher in the morn
That hope may join with tenderness
Their hearts, broken and torn.

Life is governed by its sure course,
Mother of radiant rays;
Man counts its journey in the sky
To number all his days.

Snow Showers

The sun smiles at the crispy air,
Snow flakes, like my grandfather's hair
Fall on the lady in the street
Walking slowly with frozen feet,
Wrapped up in tweed coat, scarf and hat
To buy food for herself and cat.

Today's showers are full of snow,
Woollen tufts float to earth below,
Driven like locusts, they come down
Upon foreheads which hide and frown,
Which show annoyance when they feel
Kisses from lips of icy steel.

The down scatters from the white dove,
Fingers are numb inside the glove,
The red nose hangs a drop of dew,
The mouth puffs steam from heated stew,
The young, though covered, feel the cold,
What of the infirm and the old?

White Christmas

When the winds awaken
Heaven's garden is shaken:
Its bushes wave and toss,
Observe the trees and moss,
Buildings and graveyard cross,
Then send down the candy floss.

The patches, unlike felt,
Fall down to cold earth and melt,
Then the blackness is light,
Nature is pure and bright,
The fields a lovely sight:
A carpet of brightest white.

Pure nature is glistening,
Birds to other birds listening,
But where are the field mice
As winds tighten the vice
While Winter pays their price
As they turn the snow to ice?

I recall when I saw
The white matter they called snow:
Father came from the cold,
On his shoulders a mould
That fell down in the wold
As he minded his foothold.

Soon after I discovered
That when mountains are covered
And ships sail the wide sea
Bold men go out to ski
Where ice and slope agree
As we dressed the Christmas tree.

Spring

The raging storms and tempest, their fury, at last, abated,
The earth by tears of heaven was nourished and satiated,
The roaring drums of thunder are worn out and deflated.

The bustling wind retreated before the face of the breeze,
It is time for tenderness to caress the gentle trees,
Let them sway with majesty, with splendid skill and ease.

The sleeping bud was wakened by a lonely singing bird,
It looked into the thicket from where the
squeaking was heard
To find that a new hatched life and a newborn
song were shared.

The rose washed its face with dew then slowly
opened its eyes,
Saw the sphere of shining light in blue and glistening skies,
Caused its enchanting fragrance above the
green hills to rise.

Bees, not knowing any shame, lustily kiss the flowers,
Trade fertile seed for nectar amidst the scattered showers,
Not hustled by sun or rain from dawn till evening hours.

Spring has returned, the beloved, by all nature awaited,
The day of rebirth has come, not one day belated,
Flowers greet it in the soil, in back yard walls, unslated.

Renewed nature is giving in friendship its vibrant hand,
Calling the fields and meadows, the happy
and budding land,
Asking men to ponder, behold its beauty, now grand.

The days of cold and darkness, of hardship,
severe and deep,
Retreat to allow men's dreams and fresh
hopes to gently creep
Now that life has awakened from disturbed
and restless sleep.

The Tale of Adonis

I will look for the purple heather on the hill;
I will look for the red poppy and daffodil;
They come to whisper that the winter's night is past
That the morn or reunion is approaching fast.

Time was lame when I missed you: it limped
and dragged on;
The days of lonely parting have faded and gone;
I see the fine red poppy dancing in the breeze
To welcome your homecoming, joy of lands and seas.

How deeply I sorrowed, how bitterly I cried
When your life, young and free, was slain,
perished and died.
In the snow covered meadow where you bled and fell,
The red poppy sprang with harsh nature's dying knell.

But could life ever die? You lay in mother earth
Waiting until the day when you renew your birth;
Now your feet are ready to bounce upward and leap;
Rise then with nature, refreshed by the winter's sleep.

I see your marks showing in heather on the hill,
Your beauty growing in poppy and daffodil;
I, Ashtart, am ready to keep you and to hold,
Come Adonis, for my heart never felt the cold.

Summer

The shortest day is lost in night,
The longest day comes into sight,
The sun sleeps in a bed of light.

The stars peeped early in the sky,
Now are reluctant, bashful, shy,
The full moon smiles at the firefly.

Reaching its full maturity,
Pregnant Nature, with dignity
Begets her chid, Fertility.

Golden chandeliers, green and red
Hang in vineyard and proud homestead
While wheat is ripe for making bread.

The heavy fruit weighs down the boughs,
Pastures abound with sheep and cows,
A true man thanks his God and bows.

Strolling blissfully, hand in hand,
Facing the unknown, bleak or grand,
Young lovers walk in their dreamland.

As if the whole of life is theirs,
Where are troubles, annoying cares
When the warm sun looks down and stares?

All people bless the Summer's day,
The time of mirth and holiday
And wish that it would always stay.

But when the trees shed their brown leaves
Summer feels cold without its sleeves,
It quickly packs its bags and leaves.

Autumn

It has returned to boldly say,
Farewell to warmth to Summer's day,
To herald the night on its way.

They fall, meander through the air,
They lost their grip and lost their glare,
The leaves have left the tall trees bare.

Time came to wound them and to tear,
It held them, held me in its snare
And turned to grey my ageing hair.

The sun has travelled far away,
The cold and darkness hold their sway
On man and beast and freezing clay.

Migrating birds now fill the sky,
Warbling their sombre tune on high,
Yearning for warm lands as they fly.

Come creatures, make your bed to sleep
Before the winds blow hard and sweep;
Earthworms in dungeons, hide and creep.

Many observe that life is lent,
Their numbered days are almost spent,
Foreboding strikes a spirit bent.

Sadness rises, despair is nigh,
The soul trembles as time runs by
That with all nature it will die.

Corruption marches with its woe,
Death comes to reap and plough and sow,
Even the brave will cry out, NO!

Man fears dissolution and squirms,
He will accept all offered terms,
Is the last triumph for the worms?

He clings to life with braided string,
Wonders what each new day will bring
While yearning for the scent of Spring.

Though branches break and twigs will fall,
Though death comes wearing its black shawl,
Eternity is man's last call.

Winter

As if the night has come to stay,
Tall is the darkness, short the day,
The biting wind does howl and bray.

The earth does wear a dress of white,
But when the sun sheds forth its light
Man forgets the nearness of night.

The cattle feed on bales of hay,
The grass is covered in the brae,
Horses within their stables neigh.

As if the clouds, from distant height,
Fell down upon the earth outright
To clothe the fields and trees in sight.

Some sit beside teapot and tray
Watching the fire burn away
Until the world warms one Spring day.

Man does not cease to work and fight
Against the storms and floods that blight
His dwellings with ferocious might.

He will rise up one day and pray
And plead with his Maker to stay
His hand lest death reveals the way.

Feeble his strength and great his plight
He does not know his left from right
When Nature's forces strike and bite.

He longs to see the month of May
When newborn chicks hatch out to play,
When sunshine might adorn his way.

With thoughts that give his heart delight
And dreams which feed his appetite
He whiles away the Winter's night.

The Robin

It never sang in a choir
Although properly dressed
Wearing the red shield of fire
Upon its little breast.

Its twig-like limbs are nimble,
Its hopping, firm in style;
The measure of a thimble
Sustains it for a while.

Its posture, straight, an arrow
A rocket of the skies,
And tiny bones and marrow
Add grandeur when it flies.

When men dig up their gardens
It comes with a soft chirm
Before the turned soil hardens
To snatch a wriggling worm.

When standing by a flower
It steals the splendid scene,
While in the shady bower
Excels the shades of green.

Not bound by man's religion
Yet lives by nature's creed,
A friend to the wild pigeon,
But lacks its fervent greed.

In snows of hardest winter
Picks at a lonely bough,
Its weight as on a splinter
Makes it to gently bow.

Its life is short and fleeting,
But never fails to please,
Many a Christmas greeting
Shows it midst snows and trees.

The Blackbird

Blackbird in my small garden
Who fashioned you charcoal black?
Who made your feathers glisten
That water runs off your back?
Who made your fine beak golden
To carry and pick and crack?
Your beauty ever charms me
Far greater than a greyback.

You stand in graceful manner
Looking for a hidden snare;
Much like a waving banner,
But listening to the air;
I see you timid, cautious,
Fearful to approach, to dare;
Come down, partake of plenty
While in the Almighty's care.

How deep is your chirping sound,
Almost pretending to speak!
You come for a nibbling bite

Then hurry to fill your beak
To feed your few hidden young
Whose bodies are small and sleek,
Unable to search for food
While growing stronger each week.

Who taught you art for building
A safe nest of twigs and straw
To keep your little fledgelings
From predator and foe?
When you see harm approaching,
You most assuredly know:
Your instinct flares and rises
Like a arrow from the bow.

You bring your young to visit
My small garden in the spring;
Their little feathers flutter
Excited by food you bring.
I see them grow in fatness
Till bravely they take to wing;
I hear their high-pitched squeaking:
They do their utmost to sing.

Blackbird, you go, I miss you,
Your offspring then take your place.
Where do you hide when lonely
When death submerges your face?
I fail to find your body
Amidst the branches I trace;
My God, who made and taught you,
Will keep you in his embrace.

The Fledgeling

It was crouching against the garden wall
As from its safe nest it suffered a fall,
The blackbird fledgeling seemed ready to die,
Unable to cry, unable to call.

Within five minutes it lay on the ground
With heaving breast, yet not making a sound,
It seemed that quite soon it would breathe its last,
Its short life waning, while its heart drums pound.

A moving hand approached to hold its frame
And save it from becoming a live game
To prowling cats that bite and toss and kill
A helpless creature both wounded and lame.

It suddenly moved and took to the street,
Beating its frail wings, running on its feet,
The hand chased it with skill lest it becomes
A crushed smudge of feathers and pale raw meat.

When it was captured it tried hard to bite
The hand that held it with kindness, not spite,
Which in the shade of garden shrubs it placed
The little fledgeling, overcome with fright,

And suddenly, out of nowhere, there came
A mother blackbird, like a jealous dame
That stood and stared to see whether he was
A pitying friend or a man of shame.

Nature will take its course, it is best
That one can do and leave the mind to rest,
The mother will care for it's offspring's good
And God is praised and magnified and blest.

The Moon

Arise to announce a month returned,
Circle the Earth while kingdoms are burned:
From yonder height you observed it all,
The rise of empires and their downfall.

Command the fine movement of the sea,
Of the mighty waves, seemingly free;
Cause the ebbing, flowing of the tide
In early morn and at eventide.

Then show men your young and crescent face
As in the heavens you run your race
With Venus happily at your side,
Proud to look on, unwilling to hide,

Silently rising, in silence set,
Wooing the soul to weep sand forget,
Symbol of nations in the vast East,
Signal to start the fast and the feast.

Slowly grow into a shining sphere,
Engender beauty, dispel the fear;
Guardian of lovers, guardian of love,
Light to the wayfarer from above.

Banish the starlight from the dark sky,
Climb up the mountain, ascend on high,
Preserve a corner as black as tar
Where men can espy a distant star.

Slowly diminish, then rest in sleep.
Let darkness overwhelm the deep,
Return anew to let mortal man
Number the short days of his life-span.

Worshipped by many in days of yore,
A symbol of fear and of folklore,
Yet God's laws engulf you and surround,
Your waxing, waning and awesome ground.

Your pock-scarred face awaited to greet
Man, who trampled your head with his feet;
Peering into your craters he raised
A cry from a soul truly amazed.

In lonely silence, aloof, remote,
Sail on in heaven's ocean, a boat,
Far from the noises of mother earth,
From the cry of men at death and birth.

The Universe

The stars float in the silence
Of the farthest wide expanse,
The wheels of eternity
Dance a noiseless, skilful dance,
Keep the balance of nature
In perfect, flawless stance.

They run their course faithfully
With a quartz-like precision,
Steadfast in constant motion,
Free of wayward division;
Planets circle their masses
With no chance of collision.

The fire of stunning fusions
Illuminate the vast deep:
Giant flaming tongues arise
With a bold and mighty sweep
Lick the outer edge of space
Then fall to their source and creep.

Oceans of light are seething
With a fantastic splendour;
Can language ever describe
The incandescent wonder?
Yet the timeless stars received
The force which they engender.

Masses which burst with fury
Became deserts where they lie,
Of gases shown by starlight
From furnaces far and nigh,
Like the Crab, not fully formed
Which cannot mangle the sky.

Interspersed in emptiness,
Covered in a shroud of black,
Float the gaseous nebulae
With many a hidden tack,
Riding in the endless deep
Like the Horse without a back.

The universe is finite,
Its borders are well hidden,
A shining mulberry tree
With burning fruit, forbidden;
A branch is seen in our sky,
A milk trail yet untrodden.

It spins in part and in whole
By wheels furiously driven;
Spiral galaxies, starfish
Rotate in distant heaven;
The great energy of space
Was by our great God given.

The Sea

Majesty ever rolling,
Trackless, dynamic and grand
With arms firmly embracing
Gigantic masses of land;
Here your fingers are of ice,
There of solid rock and sand;
Here men tremble, there they play
Upon your amiable hand;
In every age, every place,
Respect has been your command.

Man rides upon your body
To answer freedom's appeal,
He ventures to your bosom
With vessels structured of steel,
Greater than the mighty whale,
Unbending their stern and keel,
Hiding power, when unleashed,
That sends you to heave and reel
And can still deform the land
With blistering pock and weal.

Unbridled on the water
The merchants wallow ahead;
Man holds his soul in his hands,
Upon his shoulder and head:
Who knows into what danger
His sturdy freighters are led?
How many sank in the depths
Like giant pieces of lead!
How many souls struggled and cried
Then perished, limpid and dead!

On your backbone, your seabed
Lie many a treasures in store:
Pearls in oysters form a part
Of manifold riches, more,
Riches embossed by man's hand,
Objects he seems to adore
For which he would risk his life
To enter hell's open door.
Their wastage consumes his heart
And leaves a permanent sore.

You carried ships on your skin
Through generations past
With cargoes of slaves concealed
Beneath the deck and mast;
Some through hardship and disease
Found freedom in death, at last,
Others, dishonoured, debased
Held their ravaged spirits fast,
Then were thrown in foreign lands,
Purchased goods, helpless, downcast.

Your gentleness and beauty
Entice the sluggish to spring;
From sea shore to horizon
The sun ever seems to swing
Displaying all your splendour
That seabirds, taking to wing,
Can never match the wonder
Which your rolling waters bring;
Chords of my heart, sing with joy
As on an enchanted string.

You have been for centuries
A source of nurture and meat:
Weeds and fish of every kind
Replaced the corn and wheat,
But when you kept back your gifts
You artfully chose to greet
Fishermen whom you embraced,
Dragging down their shifting feet;
Mean, treacherous, were your deeds
Forbidding any retreat.

Is the offence real yours
When you are softer than dough?
Many sat on you shores
And let their souls feel and grow,
But when winds and storms prevail,
When savage hurricanes blow,
You are aroused to fury
To engulf in depths below
Men trusting your gentle waves
Which seemed to ripple and flow.

From the very birth of time
Awe was your offspring to be,
No man scored a winning fight,
But for mercy made a plea;
Sons of valour met their fate
Failing to escape or flee
From your bear-hug, strong and tight
Till they died on bended knee;
Sirens sounded, shrieked in vain:
Beware of the raging sea.

The Hurricane

Roll and toss, O waves of the sea,
Cover the bond slave, drown the free;
Leap like catfish into the air,
Challenge the dragon in its lair;
Twist and turn, ye wind in the sky,
Bring down the cables raised up high,
Uproot each building and tall tree,
Lift a bus as you lift a flea.
Rage, oh rage, ye heavens and earth,
Stir the foundations of your birth,
Come from the womb, behold the land
Filled with men as ants on the sand.
Roll, roll, the billows of the sea,
Cause men to die, fish to be free,
Advance a wall of warring shields,
Sound the charge and cover the fields.

Palm tree of graceful stately height,
Can you withstand the wind, its might?
When caressed by its gentle hand,
You waved with dancing to its band;

Sway not your head, but hang it down,
Else you will lose your neck and crown:
The hurricane races your way,
Prepared to overwhelm the day;
Look not upon it lest you die,
Turn your eyes from the cyclops' eye.

Destruction is left in its trail:
Earth is struck by a comet's tail,
Leaving life dying in its wake,
Sparing the fish and water snake;
Man's strong dwellings crumbled and fell,
Were carried by the rising swell.
Float woods of homes, chattels of glass,
Scattered debris on watery grass;
Men, shut your ears, the children cry
As they are washed away and die,
They fell helpless to wind and wave
Which charged the woods and mountain cave;
The fierce hurricane passed along,
Weak men trembled as did the strong.

The River

Flow, great river, gently flow
To the waiting lands below,
Through thirsty fields and meadows,
Meander as maid and beau;
Be friend to trees and shadows,
Scatter coolness as you flow;
Leave noisy, busy cities
Follow seagulls where they go.

Restore the heat-parched furrows
With moisture you bestow;
Greet the newborn grazing lambs
And whisper to them, hello!
Fill the deep vales and gorges,
Let your splendid beauty show,
Let the young trout and salmon
Increase in number, and grow.

At the dawn of creation,
Before first man used the hoe,
You nourished trees in Eden

Then standing firm row in row
And you peacefully glittered
In the setting sun aglow,
While the crystal waterfalls
Leapt with the charm of a doe.

Son of the springs in the mountain,
Of the highest peaks of snow,
Of lakes, marshes, the fountain
Where lovers learn love to know;
Born in honour, yet humbly
Working the earth lying low
Where the swan rides on your back
And the salt air breezes blow.

Undulating the mainstream
A serpent, here fast, there slow;
Waters run into your heart
To sustain the goose, the crow;
Branches spread out in the land
To bid the farmer to sow:
To trust that life will return
As in the wet sky, the bow.

Roll, mighty, ageless river,
Born many ages ago;
Let not the grassland quiver,
Rise not to become its foe;
Bring not demise, destruction,
Bring rich blessing, not the woe;
Embrace the waiting ocean,
Losing yourself as you flow.

The Volcano

The mountain stands in glory,
Resplendent and high,
Nudging the vault of heaven
Through the clouds and sky,
Hiding its dreadful fury,
Watching man and beast,
Churning its bubbling bowels
Like the hops with yeast,
Waiting in heated ferment
For its sound to rise,
Much like the roar of battle
Through the watching skies.

Waiting with bated patience,
Boiling like the broth,
It will exile the silence
In its fearful wrath.
Houses with kitchen lights burning
Live the weary day;
Men from their toil returning
Hurry on their way,

Their wives and children yearning
To welcome their eyes
As the great darkness thickens
In the anxious skies.

The dormant sun is rising
In the darkest hours,
While thunderclaps are bursting,
With blazing showers:
The sleeping giant waking
From slumber too deep,
Belches out its hot fury
On the mountain steep;
Arise, O weary bodies
From your well earned sleep,
Desert your homes and treasures
Before the fires creep.

Come, hurry up my sister,
Leave your dolls and run;
Scatter away my children
From the bursting sun:
The mountain top is melting,
With fountains aflame;
Lord, in your care abiding,
Do not blot out our name;
Great is the force of nature,
Who is strong to stand?
The molten stream gently flows
To cover the land.

Love

Her Eyes

I heard the vanquished shout a bitter cry,
I saw agony drench his heaving sigh,
Her eyes have cut his throbbing heart in twain
And sharply slashed the great superior vein.

Can any escape from their glowing fire?
Who has not fallen captive to desire?
All men were smitten when they dared and gazed,
Even the brave fell back, trembling, amazed.

I saw frozen hearts thaw, melt, burn and reel,
I saw wills bend, though made of hardened steel;
The men of might, the squadrons of the skies
Were shackled in the deep space of her eyes.

Kings and princes rushed anxiously to greet
Her smiling eyes and fell down at her feet;
They raced to war with every trick and ploy
For as great a prize as Helen of Troy.

Revealer of love buried in men's heart,
Are they bright stars or two searchlights apart?
Glowing more than fire in the sleeping night,
Heaven's lights are dimmed by their radiant light.

Fountains of crystal, great fountains of gold,
The fearful drinks and rises sure and bold,
Defies his foes in scorching heat or haze:
Her twin eyes have set his dark soul ablaze.

Jewels and pearls cannot match their splendour,
Diamonds fade before their sparkling wonder;
Only her eyes heal my pain with a glance,
Child of my wounds, slit open by her lance.

I have fallen like a hunted wild dove;
I have drowned in your vast ocean of love
Unable to flee from your hook and gun,
Dropped my weapons and found I could not run.

Your eyes speak gently, forcing me to stay
Having stolen my ravished heart away;
My flame of passion shines with ardent plea,
Will burn one day and make you think of me.

Turn not your eyes as long as mine can see
Though to their arrows I a victim be;
My spirit rushes into paradise
When it can sink into your bidding eyes.

My Queen

When brooding on the summer scene
Her shining image came between
The window and the village green.

I heard her say she loved me best
That I fulfilled her deepest quest,
For one to trust, in whom to rest.

The days floated before my eyes
When I could no longer disguise
My wish to win her for my prize.

It was in my youth and vigour
That her arrows left the quiver
To lodge in my heart and liver.

It was upon that day I swore
She will be mine for evermore,
Since her eyes pierced me to the core.

The deepest scars they left behind
Are scars of love, gentle and kind;
None but her inhabits my mind.

What is the sun compared to her?
The rounded moon that bathes her hair?
Or evening stars that peep and stare?

The stars form round her neck a lace,
The moon the dimple in her face,
The sun a shining broach in place.

Her soul is strong, joyful and fleet,
Her tender lips a source of heat,
The earth daily kisses her feet.

My heart surrendered in retreat
Long time ago when we did meet
Upon the same side of our street.

Now she is my riches and wealth
By legal right and not by stealth,
My heart's repose and my soul's health.

Her love for me will not abate,
This is what makes her truly great,
A daffodil amidst the slate.

I will never replace my queen
And in this passing earthly scene,
Only beside her will be seen.

Our Love

One moment at the break of dawn
When birds searched for a nibbling bite
And wood pigeons were heard to moan,
We felt the gentle touch of light,
We hurried through the fields of corn
And left the lonesome hours of night
Till with nature we felt reborn,
Happiest creatures in sight.

The dew had fallen on the leaves
Refreshing the long blades of grass;
The sun had not yet reached the eaves:
Concealed its face of golden brass;
Behind the great oak tree, like thieves,
Hidden from view of all that pass,
Behind the harvest wheat and sheaves
We vowed of love none will surpass.

The years vanished, as does the dew,
Trials and illness took their toll
But our love is lasting and true,

Deeper than death and life and gall,
Envy of those who thought they knew
That, like petals, will die and fall
Its beauty excels birds that flew
To heed the sunset's welcome call.

She Loved Me

Let fragrant flowers greet the air,
Let jackals nestle in their lair,
Let birds sing forth at dawn and stir:
My love said she loved me.

Stare hard, my eyes, upon her, stare,
Observe her face, serene and fair:
I fell deeply into love's snare:
Her love did arrest me.

I vowed to protect her and care,
To suffer for her and to dare,
To make her comfort my affair:
For her love did bless me.

What is life but yours to share?
With whom no creature can compare?
Give me a smile and a smile spare
When you come to kiss me.

When at my death you see me wear
The ring you gave me with a prayer,
Place with me a lock of your hair:
A parting gift to me.

Unrequited Love

It was a habit, not a spree
That she waited daily for me
In the shadow of the tall tree.

Her wide black eyes signalled a plea
While red cherry lips smiled for me;
She truly loved me, I could see,
Sinking deeper than her knee
In restless love, great as the sea.

She was pretty beyond degree,
Men would rush to her arms with glee,
Violets slept above her eyes,
Her cheeks blossomed to tempt the wise,
Were not made up to tantalize,
But were prepared to be my prize.

She walked silently by my side
Carrying shyness mixed with pride,
Careless that associates spied
And wondered if I should decide

To take her to me for my bride.
She had the courage not to hide
Her passion when she really tried
To say, she left others aside
Hoping that she will yet abide
Within my heart, loving and wide.
I felt my honour was defied.

Refreshing as the morning dew,
Gentle as butterflies that flew,
Ever scented and ever new,
Yet she never realized nor knew
My heart's desire to subdue
Gossip that I have loved anew.

How can I keep you and not be
Faithless to her who trusted me?
Who in my youth became my wife?
Whom I will ransom with my life?
She is my darling, my gazelle,
I surely would bid life farewell
And see creation play with hell
If I should lose her, or expel.
She is the nucleus, I the cell,
In the desert a living well,
Beneath her feet all beauty fell.
Her love is more than I can tell,
It is of ocean waves the swell,
Of conquering freedom the bell,
My dear, my heart is not for you,
But to my true love remains true
Though you are as gentle as the dew.

I refused her passion and plan,
I saw her weep, she turned and ran,
Swiftly married another man.

Her heart is still on fire for me,
Wishing that somehow I could be
The one who sets her being free.

Now the shadow of the tall tree
Stands alone, unguarded, free,
Without a smile waiting for me.

Farewell

My lips said, goodbye, but my heart cried, stay,
Do not uproot the sprouting buds of May;
May God protect you, ever guard your way
As you make ready to travel away.

You entered the gate to the waiting plane
As clouds rode the sky like the lion's mane;
My smile hid the fear, the longing and pain
While my soul began to miss you again.

Life, a summer's cloud in the restless air,
Passes quickly by, with frenzy or flair,
Love binds two hearts until they cling and dare
To withstand the storms that scatter and tear.

Love is life's heartbeat, feel it if you can,
Healthy nourishment for the soul of man,
Parting is sadness, none ever outran
Its striking hammer on the human clan.

Life is love's meeting, seclusion a part,
Now we are as one and quite soon we part;
I number the days of my lonely heart
Till all efforts fail to prize us apart.

Yasmeen

This terrible war snatched us part,
It left a vacuum within my heart.

I dream of you and then I find
A rough disturbance of my mind
As I wake with a sense of need
That gnaws at me with forceful greed,
Then feel regret that for my part
I did not say you filled my heart
And now I think of you and say,
Please come to me, come back today.

Had I confessed, fearless of scorn,
That when I saw you love was born,
You may have said you felt the same,
Was hoping I would make my claim
For I saw passion in your eyes
Whose gentle sparkle, never lies.

I often thought you looked for me
With shyness and with hidden glee

When you passed daily by our house
Wearing a coloured patterned blouse,
More glorious than the day's round lamp:
Beauty engraved on you its stamp.

And when we met upon the street
My pulse outpaced my nimble feet,
And while transfixed by your sweet face
My heart betrayed its urgent race,
Until I think you knew that I
Would love you truly till I die.
My courage failed to tell you that
And we would have a simple chat.
Oh, deeply, deeply I regret
That I was timid when we met.

But then we had to separate,
To live out our appointed fate,
To leave our homes and goods behind
And seek a refuge of some kind
Until the guns succumbed to sleep
And peace began to wake and creep.

I have returned, where are you now?
I must search for you, I vow
And scan the land until I see
Your face which captivated me
And tell you, though I once was slow,
I now will never let you go.

And when they told me that you died
I lifted up my voice and cried,
Then promptly asked them to explain,
They said, though bombs left many slain

Death did not come to you that way:
A sniper aimed and shot his prey.

So when I learnt that you were killed
My weeping heart could not be stilled.
O dearly loved, O dearly missed,
Your lips grew cold and were not kissed,
My soul does not know how to mend,
The stab which may herald its end.

This terrible war snatched us part,
It left a vacuum within my heart.

The Fire of Love

The scattered lanterns of the night,
The virgin moon, all clothed in white,
Hide away at the break of light.
Such is the world when you appear,
A rising sun when you are near
Driving away torment and fear.

The glowing disc is pure and bright,
Fulfils its journey in the night,
Its radiance flows from heaven's height.
The fire of love will burn and sear,
Engulfs the shadows in its sphere,
Springs from a heart like crystal, clear.

The heather of the mountain grows,
The thistle feels the wind that blows,
Stones are covered where water flows.
Such is life when you are away:
Loneliness, hardship and dismay,
Torrents sweeping all in their way.

Nothing excels the love so dear,
None can sever its roots or shear,
Gladness prevails when you are here.
And surely as life's dreams will call,
As petals lose their hold and fall,
Love sweeps all like a waterfall.

The winter days will never last,
The wild berries will ripen fast,
The spring of glory comes at last.
In life and death our love is pure,
More stable than the sun, more sure,
Will go through hell and will endure.

Come Back

Come back to my arms, your journey has been long;
Hear my yearning call while time works to prolong
The state of my mind that cannot think but long.

Who can sound the feeling? Who can understand
The effect of your love which helps me to stand,
To dispel the vacuum which I cannot stand?

You have lodged in my heart and made it your own;
Since your life merged with mine I gladly disown
My heart which you filled, which I no longer own.

What a great wonder, that one, freeborn by right,
Should choose servitude and on his soul to write:
I belong to you, more than my hand, my right?

Come back from the west, let me see your sun rise,
Be steadfast my soul, remove the gloom, arise:
She rides the morning wind and the dawn will rise.

The Stranger

They asked, why have you stayed so long
In the land where tempests are strong?
I said, I found a woman there
Who is as fresh as mountain air.

Return to your country, they said
And pick your choice from our rosebud,
If I leave her, was my reply,
My heart will wilt, my soul will die.

Sweet tenderness shows in her face:
A fine example of the race,
She grew up in the stranger's land
Where rivers flow and mountains stand.

We waited long for your return,
Have you not felt our great concern?
O wretched hour when you were sent,
How we regret the day you went.

How can you so regretful be
That I have found beyond the sea
The treasure whose like is not found
Within our land, upon our ground?

The planets ride the vault of space,
The clouds may hide their shining face,
Yet they return, alike is she,
Steadfast in love, loyal to me.

Who knows the secrets of the heart
Or what decides when love will start?
Love comes unasked to take its throne,
To make the soul its very own.

We tread strange lands and come to know
That many lives touch us and go;
Of thousands of strangers we find
Just one to love with will and mind.

To a one time stranger I call
To remain in my heart and soul,
But those who fail to understand,
Love is a stranger in their hand.

The Flirt

You plucked my soul till it was bare,
The scent of perfume in the air
Ensnared my heart and kept it there.

I truly thought that you loved me,
Your smile and soft words proved to be
A ploy to make me bend the knee.

You held me tight then let me fall,
Like picking apples in a stall
Ot bouncing hard a basket ball

All my good friends warned me of you
And bade me see the men you slew,
The way you conquer and subdue.

How can I find someone to trust
With rottenness beneath the crust
Of human nature bent on lust?

Lust to possess and to undo,
To dissect hearts and let them rue,
Not knowing folly from the true.

The day will come, it shall not fail
When it will be your turn to wail
And think of those dead on you trail.

The Dark One

Charming complexion, a shade of brown,
Tint of primordial mud and clay,
The colour which wore creation's crown
Sixth morning of creation's day.

Her hair, jet black like Arabian oil,
Shaped like waterfalls in Jizzeen,*
With wavy curl and circular coil
Glistens with a bright silken sheen.

No furrow is seen upon her head,
No plough worked by the hand of time
Pure natural silk and velvet spread
To make her countenance sublime.

Eyes, hypnotic arrows of passion,
Black as the moonless night can be,
Charm the lover to love's confession
Till he adores and bends the knee.

* Jizzeen: a city in the south of Lebanon

The flowers which bloom on tender cheek
Invite the heart to touch the bliss,
While petaloid lips, afore they speak,
Command the imprint of a kiss.

Daughter of earth, of oak bark, of fire,
Child of the East while ages run,
Men envy your colour and aspire
To paint their bodies with the sun.

Mount Hermon covers its face with snow,
Concealing its primeval earth
But the soil at its bare feet will show
Its hue upon its day of birth.

O Mother Earth, your virginal womb
Begat the line of Adam's race,
But she was fashioned in beauty's room:
Beauty rests on Melanie's face.

A Woman Betrayed

Life is wonderful, I often cried,
For it seemed glorious, dignified,
When by your embrace you verified
That I am the one you magnified.

Your lips caressed my own as they sealed
A kiss as the dew upon the field;
Our love was alive and fire did yield,
It burned all pretence, melted its shield.

You said the stars would never compare
In glory to my glorious flair,
Angels would rush from Heaven to stare,
To see how beauty gave me its share.

Queen of your soul, the throb of your heart,
Blood of your veins, of your life the start,
You vowed that you will never depart
From me, your fulness in every part.

My thoughts fly as the blackest raven,
Seeking for my spirit a haven,
Your portrait, in their web engraven.
Strengthens my hand, now weak and craven.

I was free in the spring of my life,
You wooed me gently, made me your wife,
You drank of my love when love was rife
Then turned against me with your knife.

You pierced me with an unbending sword,
Struck the hard blow as does a war lord,
My heart laments on a mournful chord,
Wilts as a dying flower and gourd.

You betrayed my soul, broke your word,
Disavowed the tender words I heard;
The sad memory that once you cared
Lingers as a treasure which we shared.

I stay awake with the starry sky,
My only love left me, tell me why?
You hug your new love, I sigh and cry,
You dare to tell me to go and die!

You gave no warning when you were gone,
Left me, a bush in the desert sun,
Awaiting the night and stars, each one,
To tell of my woe, of betrayal done.

They hear me weep and they hear me speak,
They hear me call when darkness is bleak,
They see me search for my love and seek,
Until I fall dejected and weak.

They wonder if love can turn to gall,
If sorrow can kill the soul and maul,
Because they heard my yearning voice call,
My lonely heart wail, my sad tears fall.

Where do I find him who stole my mind?
Whose heart was tender, whose smile was kind?
I trace the whole world, but cannot find
The one who went and left me behind.

I was to your life a burning fire,
Rife with expectation and desire,
But now my soul fails to rise higher,
Crawling in search of a grave to hire.

You will find the fickleness of fate,
You will be to her desire a bait,
Return to me, wide open the gate,
My love will show it is not too late.

You Left Me

Will you grow old far fro me? Will you grow old alone?
How can love, thriving and free fall as a rolling stone?
Will you pluck me from your heart where once
I reigned supreme?
Make me think it was a part of a beautiful dream.

You left me one summer's day alone in darkest night,
Carried from my eyes their ray, blinded my precious sight.
Your pride did not heed my call when bewildered and lost,
As blizzards rose to maul my life beneath the hard frost.

Time's balsam will heal the heart though silent
scars that last
Will tell that wounds cleft apart its being in the past,
They tell of love, long lost, gone, beyond he sunset far
Where birds of prey had begun to wound
your flesh and mar.

Your shadow still follows me, it will not leave my breast,
Shows you as you used to be until I cry for rest,

The thought that hurts me lingers, how like
glassware you broke,
How you slipped from my fingers,
left me to die and choke.

Now, with turmoil at your door, too hard for you to stand,
Find a little love in store, accept my helping hand,
Though you wronged me long ago and
caused the pain I feel,
I will gather strength to go and bend your heart of steel.

Waiting For You

I have grown old waiting for you,
My face has wrinkled like my shoe,
My hair turned grey,
Yet foolishly, I hope that soon
You will return with the new moon,
Return to stay.

I often thought and loudly said
That I pushed you out of my head,
But still I find:
Your image comes to haunt my brain,
To fill its caverns and terrain,
Upon my mind.

I know that now it is too late,
Years rolled and crumbled since the date
You said goodbye.
Though it is hopeless I still wait,
Burning like coal within the grate
In mid-July.

Oh, to be free, oh to forget
The joy that blossomed when we met,
Deep as the sky
And see that human love, though great,
Can perish like stinking fish bait
And putrefy.

I wish I could be strong, and free
My soul from what you were to me
In paradise,
Quit yearning after you and learn
That the volcano's heart can turn
Into black ice.

You Were

My soul is full with thoughts of you;
You were the silent morning dew
That fell upon the mountain rose
That was refreshed, blossomed and grew.

You were the sun in the blue sky
With all its glory sailing high
That gave my soul cause to rejoice
And caused my every tear to dry.

You were the poppy of the field:
Red poppy of the battlefield
That spoke of love and sacrifice
And gave comfort till wounds were healed.

You were my love, my joy, my peace,
The love that grew and did increase
Until it overfilled my soul
And was sustained and did not cease.

The moon looked down and hid its face,
The stars moved to a farther place
When they saw how your beauty caused
Their fading beauty to efface.

Your eyes, like lightning in the night
Exposed all things that were in sight,
Opened the way to the lost soul
To find its destiny and light.

And when you smiled all troubles fell,
All terrors scattered into hell,
All solace filled the heart with joy
That no one could foreknow or tell.

Such you were and will always be,
Stamped upon every part of me,
Upon my spirit and its shell
Till I succumb and cannot see.

You were the darling of my life,
The wound made by a surgeon's knife
That brings healing to the sick soul,
You were my precious Jane, my wife.

Goodbye My Love

They thought I was strong when amidst the crowd,
At home I wept and at times cried aloud,
For she knew too well that her feeble frame
Was crushed and lay beneath the darkest cloud.

A fragrant rose was thrown into the deep,
The billows surged till none could save or keep
The shattered temple of the Holy Ghost
That crumbled and fell where the shadows creep.

And yet she would smile and attempt to speak
Forming some words which she worked hard to seek
To make me follow what she tried to say,
Though her voice was low and vocal chords weak.

How I wish I knew what was in her mind,
Was it sorrow or thoughts of One most kind?
For I could not tell from her lovely eyes,
Yes, her lovely eyes that became half-blind.

Wonderful woman, most gentle and brave:
She kissed the cold mouth of the yawning grave
And boldly drank the final bitter draught
Knowing it was her Lord who took and gave.

Goodbye my love, you shall at all times be
Deep in my heart, alive and part of me.
Your face, your lovely smile and bright eyes were
Far more radiant than sunbeams on the sea.

Hiraeth

The earth was blessed wherever she walked,
The air was cleansed whenever she talked
The field crops yielded a great increase
In the land drenched by her tears and soaked.

Memories live on and cannot fail
While strong yearning and hiraeth prevail
In the mind and heart within a fort
That neither good nor ill can assail.

Her face is before my eyes each day,
Her wisdom guiding me in the way
That I should take, as I hear her words
Which keep my soul from going astray.

Hers was the love that strengthened my will,
Hers was the smile that gladdens me still,
Hers was the faith that shone in the dark
And showed me the rose and daffodil.

*Hiraeth is a Welsh word that means longing, nostalgia, homesickness, grief. It is pronounced, He rayth, the *y* as *i* in writhe, the *th* as in thigh.

They Said

They said, time heals, you will forget
The distant moment when you met
And walked upon the heavenly road
Without fear, without regret.

For she was like the morning dew:
Lingered a while and then withdrew
And she was like a long tale told
Till the dark fog hid her from view.

Then others said, the hurt will go,
As for when, you alone will know
Within a few seasons that pass
When farmers plough and reap and sow.

Yet others said, life must go on;
Journeys proceed when one is gone
Or dropped out from the long march home,
The fate of all when all is done.

Some said, she went to a safe place,
Much better than we all must face,

More happy than when here on earth,
    With no pain or fear to embrace.

Others said, she went to her Lord,
    The sure promise of His true word
    That He will take His own to Him
    In whatever method or mode.

But I still hurt and remember
    Her last breath spent that September,
    The splendid days I was with her:
    Light of my life, glowing ember.

I Am With You

And when they said to me, leave her alone
I said, my heart will die, my soul will groan,
    With her I found my place in paradise
And my true love whom I could call my own.

Thus they left and severed a life-long knot
That they proclaimed no one will ever blot,
    But time has shown that it was they who broke
A love, once deep, with a single straight shot.

What joy I had to hear her gentle voice!
What untold pleasure caused me to rejoice!
    What sacred love had bound and knit our souls:
How could one think that I made the wrong choice?

And thus we were for forty years or more
Close to each other and to Heaven's door,
    Counted as two, but we were really one:
A pattern to seek and chant in folk-lore.

It became known that love can persist,
But left alone, one struggles to exist,
Yet it was so, for time takes as it gives
And no one can outdo it or resist.

And yet, I have her with me every day,
And talk to her although she could not stay,
See her smile and hear say, I love you,
I am with you although I went away.

The Lightning

She said, let us go to the splendid field
Where the rose of Sharon grows,
Where the blackbirds sing in the trees, concealed,
Where nature's great beauty glows.

Let us see the cyclamen by the rock
With green leaves of varied hue
And there the secrets of our hearts unlock
Of our love, forever true.

As we walked gently by the field, so red
With flowers holding the dew,
She leaned toward me and most gently said,
I dearly, dearly love you.

In the foothills of the mountain one day,
With hoary head seen to glow,
We saw the mighty eagle search for prey
In mount Hermon capped with snow.

I held her tightly as our hearts did blend,
Saying, whispering her name,
Love me always and to the very end
As I surely do the same.

And thus we lived until the lightning came
And fractured the jar of clay
And left me in solitude, broken lame
With memories to portray.

Be With Me

And when the breeze with silken lace
Came to greet me and to embrace
I felt it was her fair soft hand
That touched me and caressed my face.

And when the sun stood tall to show
The wonder of rivers that flow
And mountain ranges and green hills
I heard her say, come let us go.

And when the wind began to beat
On me with a breath like concrete,
I felt her hold me as she sighed:
Remain with me, do not retreat.

And when the rain began to fall
Upon meadow and cottage wall,
Her gentle voice whispered to me:
You always answer when I call.

And when, at last, the moon did raise
Its face above me, as always
She said with a most tender kiss,
Be with me till the end of days.

Faith

Creation

"In the beginning God created the heaven and the earth" (Genesis 1:1)

Hosts of Heaven, observe and see
How time and space will come to be,
Will run their course by God's decree.

God Almighty will surely act
To form a world, perfect, intact,
With dimensions of south and north:
Out of nothing it will spring forth;
New worlds will spin before your eyes
When Earth is born with shining skies.

Blinding light emanates with might,
Shatters the darkness of the night;
It rises from its nascent sleep
To flood the blackness of the deep
And usher in the first day morn.
Particles of matter are born
Packed with energy bearing fire,
Held in a primeval sapphire
From which the seas and stars will form,
Bright green fields and magnetic storm.

Thus it was in creations sway
When light burst forth on the first day.

Winds and waves churned in the abyss,
Waited to receive Heaven's kiss
And properly divided in twain
With heaven's waters to remain
Until such time as God sends down
The Flood to cause the Earth to drown.
Thus it was in creation's sway:
Firmaments rose the second day.

Gather great waters, form the seas,
Island project, let the tall trees
Upon your multicoloured land,
Upon you naked breast to stand.
Thus it was upon the third day
That mountains, great in every way,
Towered toward the cloudless sky,
Hugged by the cold wind passing by;
Trees laden with succulent fruits
Were held by earth-bound branching roots;
Flowers of Paradise, most fair,
Distilled their fragrance in the air;
Seed-bearing plants, all dressed with green,
Sprang up to complement the scene,
While rivers coursing through the land
Caressed the rocks, the clay, the sand.
Thus it was in creation's sway:
Green Earth appeared on the third day.

Securely held by God's right hand,
Energy fulfilled His demand,
Budding forth to firmly uphold

The galaxies which did unfold.
It was when God opened His fist
That stars floated in the deep mist,
Countless as all the sea shore's sand:
Awesome power does God command!
In heaven's vault to shine from high,
The sun and moon and stars did fly;
Silently watched the world below,
Gave it their light and warming glow.
Thus it was in creation's sway:
Heaven was lit on the fourth day.

And then life in the oceans teemed:
Shark and dolphin in friendship teamed;
Whitebait, salmon and mighty whale
Swam through the weeds, dark green and pale
And in the sea the fishes breathed
While waters rushed and burst and seethed.
Then in the air birds took to wing;
They were endowed with skill to sing
And in the shades of sunlit hue
They drank of the fifth morning dew,
Their throats sounded the tunes of praise,
Their feathers gleamed in splendid ways.
Thus it was in creation's sway;
Sea and air lived on the fifth day.

The sixth day saw animals appear;
The lion, tiger, bear, and deer,
Leaping, walking with varied stance
Joined calf and lamb and wolf in dance,
Upon this novel earthly scene,
Horses trotted, cattle were seen.
It was upon the last sixth day,

That of primeval muddy clay,
God's ultimate action was wrought
When He shaped man with careful thought,
Of clay and His own breath by hand,
Upright in bearing, free to stand
And from the first day of his birth
Was made possessor of the Earth
To be to God a faithful friend,
Power, wisdom, reason to blend.
Thus it was in creation's sway:
Creation's end was the sixth day.

In this newly created world,
Wondrous beauty budded, unfurled;
Peace and harmony reigned supreme:
There was no death in land or stream;
Big fish did not consume the small:
The weeds and herbs were food for all;
Man and beasts and birds of feather
Preyed not the one on the other.

Rejoice angels, God's mighty works
Made creatures where His splendour lurks;
Who beside him can thus combine
Fission, fusion to intertwine?
Or let energy be confined
In star, insect, and human mind?
No man can ever search or know
The intricate world here below
Or heavens with their store of fire:
Who can to the great One aspire?
Thus it was in creation's sway:
God rested on the seventh day.

The Atheist's Faith

Let me tell you what happened, the atheist said,
A very long time ago when your god was dead,
And in passing, let me say, he is dead today
For he never existed, never had a say.

By chance there was mass of microscopic size
From which all known elements were to form and rise,
A dense mass of hydrogen, basis of all things,
Of minerals, gases, and life on feet and wings.
Let me interrupt, I said, do you really mean
That the weight of billions of stars could thus have been
Entrapped within a ball that could fit in my hand,
The galaxies and planets, moons and seas and land?
Yes, he said, a gaseous mass from which all things came:
Stormy skies and living things which possess a name,
The spinning galaxies and nebulae out there,
All that is in space, yes, everything, everywhere,
Mind you, I do or know how this ball came to be
But that it was there, all good scientists agree.
There was a great explosion, now called the Big Bang
And the gas scattered faster than any mustang.

The expanding universe proves that great event
Ten billion years ago, and its force is not spent
For it still expands today, fuelled with great might:
The Big Bang and not your god created the light.
No one was there to observe how it came about
But of the fact it happened there could be no doubt.

I said, you now tell me a preposterous tale
That the mass of all matter could fit in a pail,
The weight of the universe in a single ball
That was of such a size that could be graded small.

Indeed, let me tell you, this is how it began,
The gases gathered to form the children of Pan
Which all rotated around till some great chunks escaped
To form distant stars from which planets were shaped.
Our earth was such a lump that drifted from the sun
And then it cooled down as it rotated and spun.
With the passage of time some slimy mass appeared
And then life began as the molecules adhered
Each to the other forming chains, the essence of life
From their various acids which at that time was rife.
One celled-organisms divided to complex forms
Which were duly adapted to all kinds of storms
Until, with the passage of millions of earth years,
Complex life diversified in both hemispheres
Some think that life on earth started in outer space
Hitchhiking on a comet, landed in some place.

Just a minute, I said, what a fantastic tale:
An exploding fireball forms butterfly and snail
And thousands of species of insects, birds and trees,
Dinosaurs and sharks, frogs and eagles, man and fleas,

An exploding gaseous ball, given enough time
Forms a fragrant English rose and the mountain thyme,
Robin red-breast, bumble bee, lavender and lime,
Biochemical cycles, many an enzyme.
We do not fully know the functions of the cell
Nor what life really is, yet you venture to tell
That some luck and chance produced all that exists
And this process still goes on, it grows and persists.
Go, tell it to the marines, it is a great lie,
And no greater can be found underneath the sky
You indeed are a man of faith, hence you advance
Fantasies against common sense built upon chance
I believe that my God created all of this
The heavens and earth and all that in them is.

Death is Swallowed Up In Victory

Jesus came to destroy the works of the devil

A short period, soon after the birth of time
The first man stood upon the earth sublime
The pinnacle of all created life
With a free will to choose, to fall or climb.

The tempter came in a serpent's guise
With a vain promise of a precious prize,
The prize of knowledge of all good and ill
Whereby man would become knowing and wise.

The hissing serpent drew closer to Eve,
Armed with evil lies to make her believe
That they could become as wise as their God:
Such was his subtle method to deceive.

He slandered God and said that he was mean
And that his command was truly obscene,
His threats were empty and would never stand
When wisdom was waiting for them to glean.

He said, it is not true that you will die
As Death waited tensely for her reply
And when he saw that she ate of the fruit
He was excited she fell to a lie.

Now Death would not ever forget that day
When his vaunted desire would have its sway
Upon mankind and every type of life
For now he would butcher, destroy and slay.

Death entered the world through the gate of sin,
All creatures were affected and hemmed in,
It was God's judgment upon faithless man
Where no one could ever escape or win.

And thus Death reigned supreme with utmost glee
While billions of men attempted to flee
From its horrid hand, asking agent Fear
If respite be had, but Fear heard no plea.

Death in turn feared when Elijah restored
Life to the widow's son whom she adored
Until he flexed his muscles and attacked
The life restored: it was life he abhorred.

The young maid and the widow's son at Nain
And Lazarus all came to life again
When Jesus spoke a word and said, arise,
Come forth, but they died when their health did wane.

When Jesus surrendered to death a while
Death jumped for joy for his malice and guile,
But he and Satan trembled with great fear
When Jesus rose and they fell down servile.

The Lord was the first to rise from the dead
And to die no more, the saints' living head
And when he comes again, they too will rise
From death's corruption to true life instead.

Death has his sport and will punch all his blows
Until the time arrives when no one knows
When he, with Hell and Satan, will be cast
Into the lake of fire of utmost woes.

Mankind

"For all have sinned, and come short of the glory of God" (Romans 3:23).

It was as if a dream had passed
Before my wondering face,
As if my mind had floated out
Into the darkness of space
Yet could look down, view and survey
The steps of the human race,
Mind its present and see its past
In one unbroken embrace,
As if the passing of the years
Regressed in a slothful pace.

It looked as if nature was pure
Innocent, fragrant and bright,
As if mankind raped its honour
With violence and with might;
Moral darkness covered the land
That once had upheld man's right,
That once followed the way of God
Rejecting the deeds of night;
Men were locked in a fatal clasp
In a most terrible fight

Trying to shed their fellow's blood
As if they possessed the right.

Once he killed with a wooden club
Then with spear, with sword and knife;
Now he adds great rockets and guns
To destroy his brother's life
And in the darkness of the night
He steals another man's wife
As if he is driven by lust,
By wanton hatred and strife.

I looked and saw upon the street
A lady with no foothold:
She had slipped upon the pavement
Whose frozen surface was cold;
Men and women rushed to her aid
To raise her up and uphold,
To lift the fallen or broken,
To strengthen a heart once bold.
I saw some value human life
Much more than silver and gold,
Would offer their life a ransom
For a loved one, weak and old.

Yet upon the neighbouring street
A handbag is snatched away:
A woman is thrown to the ground
To become a mugger's prey.
Some fear to settle in their homes
Whether by night or by day,
Dreading that they may be attacked
By burglars who maim and slay.
I saw the poor starving for food

While rich men throw it away
And men owning other men's lives
Who beg for mercy and pray
Falling humbled in filth and dust
While violent masters bray.

Should evil or accident strike
Men rush eagerly to save,
To give solace and help to those
Unable for help to crave,
Yet nations mass out great armies
To send to a bloody grave
Thousands upon thousands of men:
Young soldiers, loyal and brave;
The bombs are thrown, people are blown,
Tall buildings crumble and cave
On all manner of men and beasts,
Not sparing the lord or knave.

How can honour and sacrifice,
Love and compassion combine
With hatred, greed and enmity
In the noble human line?
I thought there must be an answer
To unfold, expose, define
Man's notions for such behaviour
Which he falters to outline,
Then I discovered the Bible
Whose message was true, divine.

It told how the Lord Almighty
Created from simple clay
Our father, from whom our mother
Sprang into the new world's ray;

Of all the trees of Paradise
One was forbidden that day:
A simple test of obedience
That fealty may hold its sway
But they determined to rebuff,
Transgress, rebel and betray.

Death marched on a cursed universe
Till all creatures were ensnared,
None could flee its hideous power
However he tried or dared,
Evil reigned in the soul of man:
At first it pondered and stared.
Man strikes down his harmless neighbour
Yet pities a wounded bird;
Of all the creatures of the world
His fellow renders him scared,
He fails to acknowledge evil
Though at his own soul he glared
Yet God offers new life through faith
For He is a God who cared.

A Fallen World

"By one man sin entered into the world, and death by sin" (Romans 5:12).

We have traversed the burning galaxies, my friend
And have at last arrived at our journey's end.
Hidden behind the face of a middle aged sun
In constant third orbit, Earth will persist to run
Till one day it rises to ring salvation's bell
Or else be hurled to burn through the porches of Hell.
Let us now examine the living world and see
The nature of its life and fathom what might be.

What transcendent beauty adorns the high terrain
Where mountains touch the clouds above the fertile plain!
An eagle lifts a hare with deadly sabre claws
And tears it with its beak, strong as the tiger's jaws.
A life is slain so that the eagle's young may live:
The poor furry creature was unwilling to give
Its flesh for another, to be eaten alive:
Vainly did it struggle and vainly did it strive!
Further down the mountain there lies a bright red stain
Of a savaged grazing lamb that the wolf had slain.
Oh what raging violence! Let us go elsewhere
Till we discover hope beyond this dark nightmare.

Rumbling guts belch out the fire from a volcano's mouth
In the hard frozen north and the temperate south;
Earth's shoulders are shaking, as if rising from sleep
While ocean beds collide with each other and creep
Bringing havoc and fury that destroy and maul
Creatures buried in dark pits as soon as they fall.
Disaster tops disaster: death's fangs are unfurled,
Jaws and beaks drip with blood, agony fills the world.

The Earth's mighty oceans, many a trackless sea,
Contain vigorous life, roaming, seemingly free,
But in the deep waters the strong devour the weak
While the howling whirlwind nudges the island's peak;
Who can stay its power? It fiercely comes this way:
Churns the wind of heaven as darkness rules the day,
Yet the valiant human attempts to ride the storm:
Is his life a struggle, calamity the norm?
Let us hurry skyward until the storm is spent,
Then return to find out if he is straight or bent.

He stands upright, not crawling upon foot and hand,
Unlike creatures looking down when they fly or stand,
He, with his skilful hands, forms his own creation,
Child of a fertile brain which rejects frustration.
We escaped his rocket reaching the outer sky,
A mark of his genius that never fails to try.
He traverses the Earth in his flying machines,
Sails the sea, digs the land, conquers the deep ravines;
Let us observe if life has smiled on him or frowned
For upon the planet no equal can be found.

Hear her cry of lament: her stillborn is well formed,
Hear her weep in the night: her baby is deformed;
That bereft mother wails: within her womb he died,

His life could not return however much she cried.
Watch him in the prime of youth, stricken by disease,
Breath hanging on a string with no comfort or ease;
Pain strikes the nerve endings as lightning strikes the skies,
The soul is crushed, tears fail to solace when it cries.
The old man, confined to bed, cannot rise and walk
Nor attend to himself, with face as white as chalk;
The woman in the street, with stick and shabby dress,
Falls victim to a car, becomes a black red mess.
Man's days seem insubstantial, as dust in the pan,
Death waits outside his house to shorten his life span,
At times it is demure, and knocks his wooden door,
At times, with violence, slays him upon the floor;
Few are strong to face it, most men will weep and cry,
Knowing its certain demand, yet they fear to die;
Man is one by nature all men are born to die,
All men are born to suffer, all men are born to cry.

See what splendid honour man shows in every way
While he suffers hardship and seeks those gone astray;
He bears pain and hunger to feed his little ones,
Defies untold danger, the nozzles of the guns.
He climbs up the rock-face to save one trapped alone,
Knowing a fall will cause the breaking of each bone.
Even in the ocean he takes the stranger's side
Though the sharks may slay him, the fury of the tide.
Life hangs in the balance, he struggles for his kin,
Health may fail, advancing age creases up his skin.
Man is a great wonder, most noble, true and wise,
Who could wish him evil or witness his demise?
Look, he charged the lion so that his child may run,
He is mauled and dying in the harsh blazing sun.

What are those rising clouds, hovering thick and black?

Unlike the clouds of heaven, no lustre fills their back?
They are signs of tumult, of men engaged in war
Where the rockets shatter the living by the score.
Thousands of explosives litter the burning sky,
Fall upon the cities, thousands of people die
While in alleys and houses, slaughter and rape are done,
Bellies opened, heads smashed, no one escapes, not one.
Is this an exception that man performs such deeds?
Have we not seen him suffer for his fellow's needs?
Let us search the whole Earth for the subtle answer,
A play cannot be judged by a single dancer.

In cities, in jungles, the story is the same,
Culture lends him no escape from this evil game.
Man cannot rid himself of what he is inside,
His venom is spat out with defiance and pride.
He boasts of hurtful deeds, rewards his fighting men,
Leaves the weak and poor like a disembowelled hen;
Look not on his actions, he is worse than the beast:
It kills to feed hunger, but he to gloat and feast,
Master of the Earth he keeps creatures in his grasp
But in his heart there lies the poison of the asp.
He could not conquer greed nor lust and love of fame
Nor overcome his desire to build himself a name.

Look at that young woman, she gave body and mind
While he seeks another, and another to find,
Casts his children away to dire hardship and need,
To gratify his lust, he spits upon his seed.
One, for love of money, betrays his closest trust,
Plotting with skill and craft to place men in the dust.
Mass murder is performed on progeny unborn
Where in their mothers' wombs they are
destroyed and torn.

Yes his moral nature is lesser than the brute:
He uproots his own kind and of the womb the fruit.
Man stood upon the moon and sent spaceships above,
Yet cannot live on Earth and show sufficient love.
Let us investigate if this has always been
And look into his past to see what could be seen.

Structures of past ages are scattered in the lands,
On the mountains and greens and in desert sands;
Skyscrapers nudge the sky in a proud upward drift,
Like ancient monuments show a genius' gift,
But the tale is of war, of bloodshed from times past,
Of conquerors and slaves, of glory running fast,
Of tales of one who wept when naught was left to spoil,
While the blood of innocents drowned the thirsty soil.
Though man's learning has increased, within his
heart is found
Spreading roots of enmity, cruelty unbound.
Man is a paradox, possessing good and ill,
His reason and desires support a wayward will,
Meets death for another, yet another betrays,
Strives that life be preserved and then butchers and slays.
The fury of nature lasts for a brief moment,
Calm follows howling storms, but man creates torment,
Millions fell to his bombs, to his swords and rockets,
Heads fell down, throats were cut, eyes
removed from sockets,
But the sea and mountain, the free wind of the storm
Raged to claim a thousand of life of every form.

Like a lost ship adrift, far from the peaceful dock,
Life is steered by evil against a mighty rock
And in the deepest darkness the soul of man will grope
Till he walks in God's way, his only certain hope.

Did the wise Creator make this planet to be
A home for snakes, scorpions, and deadly enmity?
Violence rules creatures, the entire life-filled world:
This Earth has earned Hades: therein it may be hurled.
Come to the beginning, search what the Lord has made
Ere the day when Adam betrayed his God and strayed.

He walked with his Maker in a garden of trees,
Of beauty and riches, made to nourish and please,
Clad with splendid features and fine moral stature,
Was made warden of Earth, of its ordered nature,
When the Devil tricked him, disaster struck them all,
The ancient Book recalls what man now calls the Fall.
Death and ill stormed the world and became his lot,
Corruption in his frame, sin on his soul a blot.
Man, like his monuments, shows relics of his past
When he walked with God and kept his goodness fast.

Here, there, in the darkness shines a flickering light:
Men are born of God's life and rescued from the night.
Yes, a great mystery took place upon this Earth
When our Lord, most humbly, received His human birth.
We look with wide wonder upon this stretch of soil
To see where man's Saviour, with His blood did foil
The work of the Evil One so that one day the morn
Of a new world and Earth will be truly reborn.

Let us return swiftly through the fulness of space
And report that evil is rampant in this place,
See in our Maker's hands His scars of matchless grace.

Blind Bartimeus

"And Jesus stood still and, commanded him to be called" (Mark 10:49).

Ttimeus' son sat on the street
To beg for alms of coins and meat,
To plead for handouts, ask for bread
While flies explored his face and head.

He begged when he lost his eyesight
And missed the guidance of the light;
He could do nothing else but cry
And seek pity from passers by.

The Saviour passed, there was a sound
As rushing crowds gathered around;
The blind man saw his chance at hand
And shouted like a roaring band.

The crowd told him to shut his mouth
And not be like a blabbermouth,
But Jesus heard his shout for help,
The shout of agony, a yelp.

"David's son, have mercy on me";
The Lord stood still: He heard his plea;
'Bring him to me' was His reply:
No entreaty from Him must die.

"He calls for you", the people said,
"A guiding hand leads you ahead";
The man threw all hindrance away
With frenzied zeal to find his way.

"I need no riches, please be kind,
Pity me Lord, for I am blind,
Restore the sight of my dark eyes
That I may see green earth, blue skies".

The tender Lord was never slow
To pity one whose tears did flow;
The blindness vanished with a word,
The sound of praise could then be heard.

O Lord, the weight of sin makes blind
The heart of man, his will and mind;
Send out Your word to give new sight
To those who live in darkest night.

Bethlehem

"There was no room for them in the inn"
(Luke 2:7).

The inn is too crowded, the night is enshrouded
By a mantle of deep black;
I think I can help you, may Heaven defend you,
Oh, how can I turn you back?
Please go to the stable, your donkey is able
To feed on the straw and hay
And there, with God's creatures of familiar features,
Shelter through the night and day.

God has prepared our way, opened our path today,
Come Miriam, heavy with child;
Come rest beneath the roof, not in the fields aloof
Where ravenous beasts run wild;
Far from the noise of men, the tumult of the den
Your travail will not be heard,
The cattle will stand by and will not mind your cry
Nor will they fret and be scared.

Through God's mercy indeed, the governor decreed
To usher salvation's morn,
The prophets long foretold: in Bethlehem of old

The Redeemer will be born.
Our Lord rules over all, the heathen heed His call
And act His story so well,
The creation did long for one who will be strong
To deliver it from hell.

Condescension

"And the Word was made flesh, and dwelt among us" (John 1:14).

And were you born like other sons of men
With blood and water on your crinkled skin?
And was the sound of praise to God heard when
You breathed and cried in the cave of the inn?
And did you suckle on your mother's breast
And crawl upon your little hands and knees?
Great God who spread the sky from east to west,
Whom angels praised and delighted to please.

And did your mother hold you by the hand
And teach you how to walk and dress and speak?
And did you fall, not knowing how to stand,
Who made man's feet to sprint, his tongue unique?
And did you preach to men the word of life,
Calling them to repent and turn to God
While they despised you, urging you to strife
And said that you served in the devil's squad?

And did you see the soldiers passing by
With slaves in chains, ill clad, wounded and sore?
Till they were raised upon crosses to die

Ravaged by pain, bearing their sweat and gore?
You saw and knew that this will be the lot
You must endure to do your Father's will,
That you would bear man's sin and every blot
By tasting death upon that lonely hill.

And did they lay you on a slab of stone
And wrap you tightly with a linen cloth?
Until you rose from the dark tomb alone
And showed that God has turned away His wrath?
The mystery of mysteries must be
The Shepherd died to gather His sheep in
That Christ the Lord was born a man for me
And gave His life for the vile creature's sin.

When Jesus Died

"The veil of the temple was rent in twain...the earth did quake...and the graves were opened..." (Matthew 27:51,51).

When Jesus died the earth strained at its mooring,
Creation reeled as if it quit enduring,
The land convulsed and by shaking had spoken
That Earth's frame bent when its Maker was broken.

Well might the stars have left their lofty stations
And galaxies fell from their sure foundations,
The universe burnt, bursting and colliding
Had not the Father kept all things abiding.

The angels gazed, bewildered, crowding, stooping:
Their Creator died, His holy head drooping,
The sun wore black, the world's Light was extinguished,
A lonely man, but totally distinguished.

But just before, all Heaven quaked and trembled,
Angels were startled where they all assembled,
His shout pierced the skies while the pillars of Hell
Moved and swayed and cracked as they crumbled and fell.

When Jesus died the Devil laughed and bleated,
Thinking that God was finally defeated,
Saints left their graves, a wonder signifying
That Christ's death brought life to the dead and dying.

Now God receives men under condemnation
Whom justice claimed for unceasing damnation,
The way to Him was opened and made certain
When celestial hands tore the Temple's curtain.

Raised by the Spirit, the Lord then ascended
To Heaven in view of men He defended,
Death's ravage by Life was part of His story
Which He will complete when He comes in glory.

The Tree

I will speak of what multitudes know
Of a tree which flourished long ago
Before making of paper was known
Or fields were mechanically sown.

From seedling to a giant it grew
Adorned by green leaves of every hue,
While pregnant branches carried hard fruit
Nourished by the water seeking root.

When clouds vanished and heaven was blue,
Its leaves collected the drops of dew;
The weary farmer rested his head
Beneath its shade on the earth, his bed.

Did Jesus once lean against that tree?
Against its strong stem, His cross to be?
And shelter from the heat of the sun
Before His earthly journey had run?

Land birds perched on its arms to rest
Prepared for their new fledglings a nest,
While at its fallen decaying leaves
Men could observe how the spider weaves.

No boat was built of its wood, no ship
To float in the sea and roll and dip;
No house or palace or wooden shed
Possessed from its skeleton a bed.

But from its branches, fallen and torn,
The amber flame was often reborn
Where men slumbered and let their minds stray
To muse on the events of the day.

One morning the tree fell to the axe,
It was transported upon mules' backs,
Was nailed to another, freed from moss,
To build a lonely reclining cross.

Upon its limbs, now barren and dry
The Son of God was to bleed and die;
Man cuts the tree in mountain and plain
To hang his fellow to die in pain.

Christ wrought with chisel, hammer and plane
Excellent works, respecting the grain
Nazareth's carpenter matched the wood
Till articles of perfection stood.

Sometimes I ask, did He ever place
One beam across another's face
Then ponder upon the solemn price
He was to offer, the Sacrifice?

Symbol of increase, or fruition,
Of slow torture in man's tradition,
Symbol of death and damnation
Is symbol of life and salvation.

The Crucified

It was in the garden of Gesthemane
Where Christ the Saviour sorely wept
As His disciples slept;
Where men, like thieves, against Him crept;
There, He knelt and fervently prayed
Until the hour He was betrayed
For thirty silver pieces, paid
By men who judged they could afford
To pay for Him a mean reward.

The moon had hid away its light,
The sun removed its robes of white
Crickets broke the silence of night,
As He struggled away from sight
In the garden of agony,
Where His sweat drops, like rubies, fell
To speak of His sorrow so well,
Of whom the Scriptures did foretell
He will break the power of Hell
By his deep pain and agony.

The crimson from His brow did flow

Through torment, only He could know.
Many a man would die with pride,
Despise the gallows and deride
While heartless men will gloat and chide.
Bruised by whips of animal hide,
His feet stumbled, He could not stride
As He carried His cross and tried
To keep it on His back and side
While Satan's hosts hurried to ride
To see that Christ was crucified.

His anguished heart was free from fear
That hardened men would jeer and sneer,
Or that His blood will smear His skin,
But that His soul will bear man's sin
When guilt was laid on him that day
So that His Father looked away.

Who knew pain as the Crucified?
Who felt His soul putrefied?
Not even the thieves mortified,
Who for their deeds of guilt had died.
He rent the Heavens when He cried:
Water and blood flowed from His side.

On Calvary's cross of dire shame,
Life is dead, the light-footed lame,
Victims are deemed sport for the game;
None could boast his pedigree or name.
Men, with fervour, mock the dying,
Laughter, mirth and jokes supplying
With raised voices, God defying:
No pity when a body fails,
Hands feeling the bite of the nails.

What mind can ever try to sound
God's wisdom on Calvary's mound?
The hill, the battlefield for man
Where Hell's demons to battle ran
And were defeated in their plan
And man is saved by Christ the Man.

The Lord of life, creation's head
Gave His life for the living dead:
A sacrifice of awesome dread.
Of His pleasure He came to save
Men whom evil did once enslave
In its darkest dudgeon and cave.

Their risen bodies will yet fly
To their great Redeemer on high
When this Earth turns to fiery red,
When graves throw out their silent dead,
When the Lamb is the Judge instead.
Christ rose triumphant from the dead,
He did leave His burial bed,
The bed of stone on which He stayed
Where His shrouded body was laid
Until He crushed the Devil's head.

Who could think, that on a dry tree
God would release the sinner free?
It is the greatest mystery.
Once He determined to save man
He set to accomplish His plan
To pardon sin and save the soul,
Make ransomed men and women whole;
They are His treasure and His prize,
His home is theirs beyond the skies.

Repentance

Weary my soul, my mind, my heart,
I lay on You my sadness,
Refresh me like a newborn hart
That leaps with joy and gladness.

My soul is laden like a cart:
A bridled mule in harness;
Come to my aid, give me a start
Out of the mire and darkness.

Hell bound by sin, yet torn apart,
I cry in pain and weakness;
Come, cleanse my soul in every part
To taste of grace the sweetness.

Forget the sins of my dark past:
In Christ I plead forgiveness;
Make me Your own while life shall last
To live and praise Your greatness.

Loneliness

"Then all the disciples forsook him, and fled (Matthew 26:56).

Jesus struggled when facing the great flood
Of sin and death, and sweated drops of blood;
His friends left Him to pray alone to God
While they slept, while they slept.

He was arrested as the torches blazed
While His disciples stood dumbfounded, dazed;
For just a moment they pondered amazed
Then they fled, then they fled.

The lonely lamb then faced a vicious pack
When injustice and envy showed no lack
Of violence as soldiers rent His back
With a whip, with a whip.

He bore it in silence, no tears were shed
Though the stripes were fierce and His body bled;
They spat upon His face and crowned His head
With the thorns, with the thorns.

No one was present who could understand
From the raging crowd or the soldiers' band
Why Jesus gave Himself, stretching each hand
For the nails, for the nails.

All this was nothing to truly compare
With His deep torment which no man could share
That God, His Father, could not look or stare
At His Son, at His Son.

Each of us wondered, like a sheep has strayed;
Each ruffled his bed of sin where he laid,
Yet for these sins the awful debt was paid
With His blood, with His blood.

Christ Conquered

He stared at death with flint-like courage
Submitting to unmeasured shame,
While men flocked from city and village
Eager to murder and defame.

Shouting as in the day of pillage,
Howling like blood hounds for the game,
They gave their King for Rome to savage
Though Pilate found in Him no blame.

The blackness of hell marred His visage
When sin was laid upon His frame,
For Jesus the Lord paid His homage
To death for those He chose to claim.

He suffered with the certain knowledge
That Death will flee before His name;
Hell and Satan could not envisage
Their servile action in His aim.

Death was killed and in the ravage
Satan was bound, helpless and lame;
All people shout out loud the message:
The Christ conquered and overcame.

For Me

The Son of God, who loved me and gave himself for me" (Galations 2:20).

For me, for me you came to die
So many years before my birth;
The anguish of your dying cry
Pierced through the heavens and the earth.

Your skin was torn, your body bled,
The nails transfixed you to the tree;
God's vengeance fell upon your head
As you suffered and died for me.

Great darkness fell upon the land:
Transaction between God and Man
Was certified by God's own hand;
Salvation wrought for sinful man.

But yet the Lord was pleased to slay:
His holy wrath was satisfied;
You paid my ransom on that day:
The way to God was opened wide.

Your friends escaped, your mother wept,
You faced hell's agony alone
Before you tasted death and slept
And rested on a slab of stone.

The chains of death could not hold fast
The Prince of life, the meek and brave;
God's Spirit, true from first to last,
Raised up the Christ from the dark grave.

Praise be to God, the One in Three,
The wisdom, sacrifice, the might;
To you shall my obedience be
Till faith is transformed into sight.

Salvation

"The Son of God was manifested, that he might destroy the works of the devil" (1 John 3:8).

With heavy chains he drowned in sin
And did not seek a chink of light;
Rebellious pride settled within
His blighted soul, slave of the night.

Lost was the day of pure delight
Which was his at the dawn of time
When man was holy in God's sight
Before Adam acted his crime.

Deep in the cave of sin he lay,
No hope to cheer a spirit bound
Until the Saviour won the day
And lifted his soul from the ground.

The time was ripe for the great fight:
God, clothed in flesh, stood on the earth,
Wielded His righteousness and might
And freed the sinner by new birth.

The battle for the soul of man
Was fought by man, yet God the same
And though the foe took flight and ran
Yet he was crushed before His name.

Glorious the Lord for sinners slain
For in His blood is life and balm;
Satan can never rise again:
Is chained forever by the Lamb.

Sing forth the song of victory:
The Christ has won the life of men;
Great is the God of mystery,
The God of sea and hill and fen.

Like Seagulls

Lord of heaven and earth and sea,
Hear my fervent prayer and plea,
Bless my loved ones, remember me,
Please help the needy refugee.

Scattered like seagulls upon the sand
Far from our home and motherland,
Let us each one persist to stand
With grace and favour from your hand.

With lonely hearts we face the day
Bowed as the wind on standing hay;
O God, our only strength and stay,
Keep us secure, turn not away.

Open our eyes that we may see
The Lamb of God upon the tree;
Save us from bondage, set us free:
Our praise shall rise eternally.

Dishonoured

Dishonoured was He beyond degree
And was nailed to the wood of the tree,
Two thieves were His companions to be
When Jesus suffered on Calvary.

What really happened on Calvary?
Upon that middle cross of the three?
The Lord of life, for you and for me
Surrendered His life to set us free.

He lifted our burden: we must flee
To the Saviour upon bended knee;
The day is coming when I shall see
The scars of His wounds that bled for me.

Death of a Christian Lady

Death came to share a woman's bed,
He was dismayed he caused no dread
When his proud chest and hands were red
With blood from those who ran and fled.
Though cancer grew in her and spread,
Death was her slave, it will be said,
For he could see his pathway led
To Heaven, to Christ, her living head;
Death wails that glory lies ahead.

He saw her, then began to snore,
Weary of plucking field and shore.
He will leave her a few days more,
She might beg him upon the floor,
For he regards himself at war
With her spirit, until his roar
Will frighten her soul to its core.
Till then he had a plan in store:
To knock hard at the neighbour's door.

Many people, in such a state,
Will accuse God and curse and hate.
It is the lot of man, his fate
To meet his death, however late.
The grave consumes humans like bait,
Its hunger grows, will not abate,
It cries when men enter its gate
Through murder, war, or simple freight:
Bring more, bring more, I hardly ate.

With weakened body and thin hair,
She will fall into death's dark lair
To be a part of what men share,
But in the twilight she could bear
And knew that she will surely stare
On Him who wrapped her in His care.
Her body will rise from the snare
When Jesus comes back in the air
To tell the dead, rise up and stir.

Though nearing the end of her race,
She wanted news of God's good grace,
Of those who once lived in disgrace
And now are found in Christ's embrace.
Since Christ has died, no man is base,
No virtue gained through birth or race:
Each must mind God and seek His face.
Should death speed up his slothful pace,
Heaven will be her resting place.

Her friends sang hymns, Scripture was read,
They praised the Christ who died and bled,
Whose life was offered in their stead.
Death shall in Hell ruffle his bed;

For them there is new life instead
And resurrection time ahead.
But they missed her and tears were shed
And in deep sorrow bowed the head:
Showed how Christians bury their dead.

Christ Will Remember

Ponder the experience of man:
Turmoil and pain, struggle and toil
Faces driven into the soil,
Smudged into the filth and dirt
By greedy men, scourge of the earth,
Self-sufficient lovers of mirth
Until the poor begin to flirt
With death that it may lose its way
And take its hideous face away.

Men, with a mighty boastful hand
Crush the feeble with studied boots
And pluck him from his very roots;
They scatter him across the land
And treat him lesser than the brutes.

Children are born and children die,
Young men grow old, women will try
To hide time's hand with painted face:
Crumbling bones beneath silken lace.
The span of love and joy will last

Till disappointment, lie a worm,
Nibbles the weak heart and the firm
And men are like refuse outcast.
Though strength will flourish for a while,
It fades as fades a put-on smile:
The years disable all who live,
Who try to buy what life will give.

And in the darkness of the tomb,
Black as the blackness of the womb,
The mind is blind to every sight,
Sense organs cannot sense the light,
Ears are deaf to the sound of life:
Thunder of canons, shout of men
In agonizing fight with death
While babies cry amidst the strife
Their bellies like a vacant den,
Crying until time stops their breath.
Then they will fall into the grave
To join the scoundrel and the brave;
They could not tell the day from night,
Nor comprehend crawling and flight,
Yet they will share the fate of man,
Discarded like an empty can.

In such a state, early or late,
Devoid of love, empty of hate,
I ask if faith can see beyond
The fiery lake and limy pond,
Burst to life like leaf and frond
And bid eternal life respond?
Will it reject dollar and yen
And scatter hope to dying men
Before wriggling worm, slimy slug

Creep on the graves with snail and bug?
Will it yet ask when life is dead
And corruption like cancer spread,
Will Christ the Lord remember us?

We share the throes of earthly woe:
Stinking bodies reduced to bones
Hidden beneath the clay and stones
Where eye sees not or brains dare know
How men break up like melting snow,
Or seething sea that will enmesh,
With weeds and worms the rotting flesh.
Then with the passing of the years
Men will forget their wailing tears
That on the open grave once flowed,
For time will send its healing balm
To fill the mind with soothing calm
Like clouds that gather and unload
Their rain upon budding flowers
Where snails wake up in the showers:
Memories fade upon life's road.

Some will remember till they die
Their loved ones who succumbed and went,
Whose numbered days were wholly spent.
The flood of tears may one day dry:
Their voices call, their spirits cry
For those upon whom time has sent
Its gleaming axe till they were bent.
They will recall, yet One remains
Whose effulgent life never wanes:
Jesus the Lord will not forget.
He shall raise our bodies anew,
Fresher than morning air and dew,

Of decomposed earthly remains,
Or mouldy lungs and mouldy brains
Which hold the bones, the bloody stains
Of the dead beneath the amber;
Yes indeed, Christ will remember.

The Last Day

"The trumpet shall sound and the dead shall be raised" (1 Corinthians 15:52)

Tremble at the last trumpet's call,
Down on your face, begin to crawl;
Are you mighty enough to stand
As you enter the judgment hall?
God comes to sentence and command
All the rich and poor of the land.
Approach all men, the great and small,
Release your dead, ye desert sand,
The day of judgment is at hand,
Its sight and sound will make you fall.

Cast out your dead, ye raging seas,
Return the souls you felled like tree;
Have you not heard trumpets calling?
All life within you will now cease.
Have you not seen mountains falling?
The sight of the end appalling?
Roll your white billows as you please,
Stop, ye ships begone your trawling,
Time has ended, no time for brawling:
Ye dead, kneel down upon your knees.

Ashes born in the flames of fire,
Restore your dead men from the mire;
Ashes scattered into the air,
Remake the old and worn out sire;
Form the visage of young and fair
In Indus valley and city square.
Valiant men, builders of empire,
Will your unbending steel hearts dare
Into God'd holiness to stare
Having kindled many a pyre?

Turn your eyes, you cannot look:
Your heart is as the blackest rook;
Your evil deeds shall be outspread
When God will open Heaven's book;
Your sins which were your drink and bread
Are part of you, on them you fed;
Your spite flowed as a Winter's brook;
Lament aloud, hang down your head,
Utter darkness shall be your bed
With those who said, God will not look.

Rise up and flee, the hour has come,
Drown yourself in gin and rum;
Will you shelter beneath the ground?
You will see of your deeds the sum.
Close your ears to the painful sound,
Rising as the squeal of the hound:
The wailing cry, the moaning hum
Of men whose glory was earthbound,
Whose boastful words did once resound,
Reared in palace and reared in slum.

Earth will burn with a great burning:
Ended are research and learning:
The world, by evil polluted,
Will halt its spinning and turning;
It will be plucked out, uprooted,
Till its shameful cry is muted.
Heaven, with its new adorning
Of just men, prepared and suited,
Whose life in their God was rooted,
Will glory in a new morning.

Lord, I fear for men and women
Who will not partake of Heaven;
While I bless You for salvation,
I wish they could be forgiven.
Men from every tribe and nation
Have escaped the condemnation.
I quake at the sentence given
On those marked out for damnation
With no hope of restoration
When into hell they are driven.

Almighty God, send down Your grace
On the lost of the human race.

Evening Prayer

O Lord, the night draws to enclose
Our souls, ready for deep repose,
As now, in sleep, our eyelids close,
Watch over us, Heavenly Father.

Almighty, whose eyes never sleep,
Guard my loved ones as shadows creep,
Comfort the sad who mourn and weep,
Heal their wounds, Heavenly Father.

Look down upon us through the night,
Let no nightmare or ill affright,
Let our thoughts be holy and right,
Give us dreams of Heaven, O Father.

Support the poor, restore the weak,
Uphold the pure, sustain the meek,
When we are lost, let us all seek
The way that leads to You, O Father.

Be with the men upon the seas,
Refresh them with the gentle breeze,
Let all danger banish and cease,
Come to their aid, Heavenly Father.

Remember those who soon will die,
Let them in their sickness rely
Upon Your mercy to supply
Eternal peace, Heavenly Father.

Think of the bereaved, lonely, old,
Be to them more precious than gold,
Make their spirits steadfast and bold:
They have no other help, O Father.

Forgive the sins of this past day,
The unkind words that we did say;
Humble our hearts in every way
To live for You, Heavenly Father.

Grant our bodies a quiet rest,
Let us be numbered with the blest,
Be strong on our behalf and wrest
Our souls from outer darkness, O Father.

Should You call our spirits to be
In Your presence, happy and free,
We cry aloud on bended knee,
Uphold those who remain, O Father.

Morning Prayer

For rest in sleep throughout the night,
The hand which held us with its might,
For singing birds that greet the light,
We praise Your name, Heavenly Father.

That the pain subsided as we slept,
That comfort reached us as it crept,
For mercy which healed us and kept,
We give You thanks, Heavenly Father.

Give us the courage to face the day,
Show us the pitfalls in our way,
Guide us in all we do and say
That we may honour You, Heavenly Father.

For those with a broken spirit,
Subdued, failing to inherit
Solace in Christ and His merit,
We pray for heavenly joy, Father.

Some find this life a heavy load,
Hunger and sickness pierce and goad,
Send them sustenance along the road
And rest in You, Heavenly Father.

The widow, the orphan the poor,
Whose troubles seem to have no cure,
The oppressed who cannot endure,
We pray for them, Heavenly Father.

Your children on the sea and land,
All my loved ones, fed by Your hand,
Be their support that they may stand
In life and death in Christ, O Father.

Let all men praise You and extol,
We gladly surrender our all,
Let us see the gates of Hell fall
Before your Christ, Heavenly Father.

About the Author

Salim Khalil Haddad was born in Palestine of Lebanese parents. He studied Medicine and Surgery in the universities of Cambridge and London and specialized in Neurosurgery in London. He is now retired and lives in Wales, United Kingdom.

www.ingramcontent.com/pod-product-compliance
Lightning Source LLC
Chambersburg PA
CBHW051722040426
42447CB00008B/932